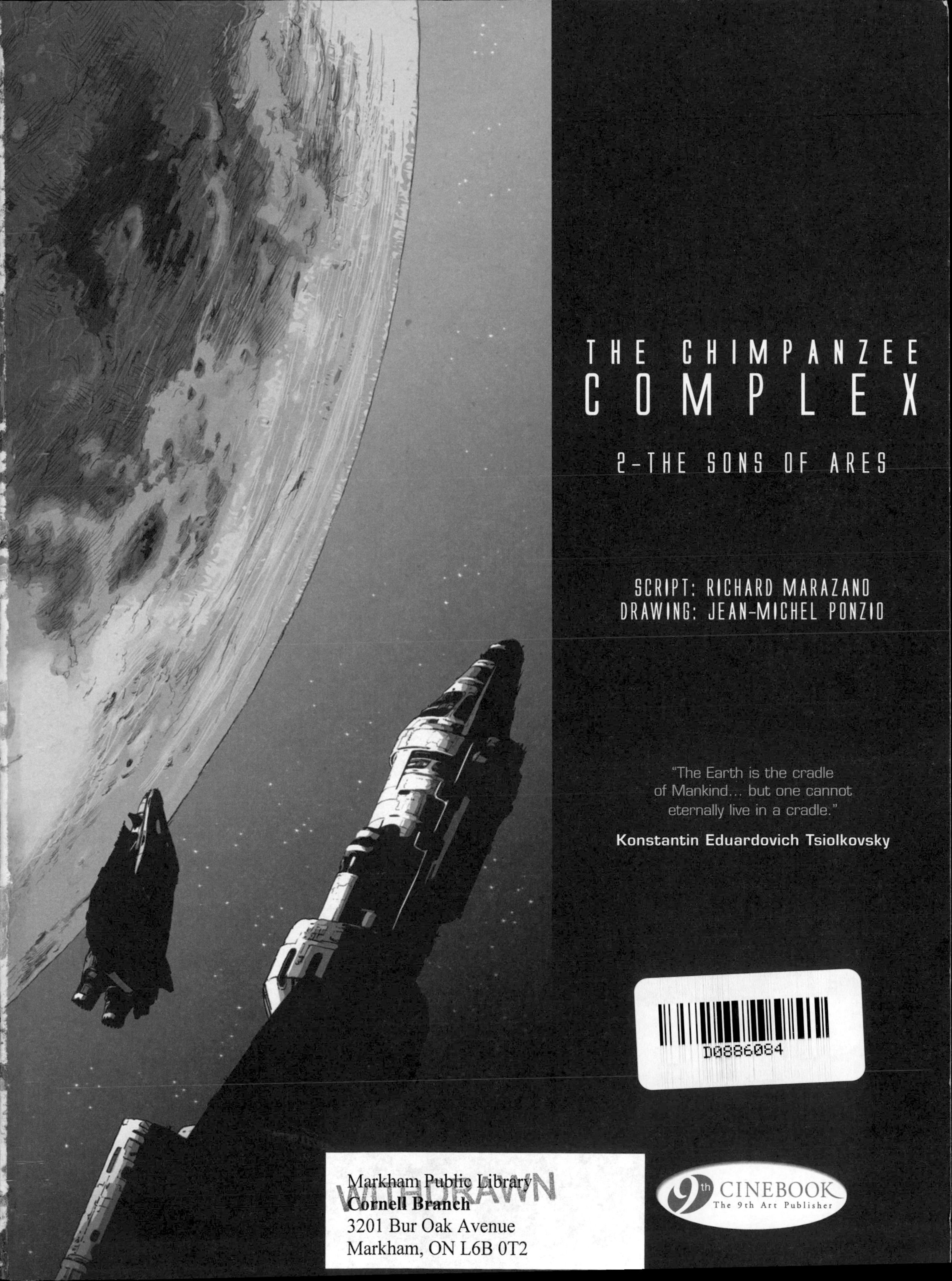

THE CHIMPANZEE COMPLEX

2 - THE SONS OF ARES

SCRIPT: RICHARD MARAZANO
DRAWING: JEAN-MICHEL PONZIO

"The Earth is the cradle of Mankind... but one cannot eternally live in a cradle."

Konstantin Eduardovich Tsiolkovsky

9th CINEBOOK
The 9th Art Publisher

Original title: Le complexe du chimpanzé – Les fils d'Arès

Original edition: © Dargaud Paris, 2008 by Marazano & Ponzio
www.dargaud.com
All rights reserved

English translation: © 2009 Cinebook Ltd

Translator: Jerome Saincantin
Lettering and text layout: Imadjinn
Printed in Spain by Just Colour Graphic

This edition first published in Great Britain in 2010 by
Cinebook Ltd
56 Beech Avenue
Canterbury, Kent
CT4 7TA
www.cinebook.com

ISBN 978-1-84918-015-3

9th CINEBOOK
The 9th Art Publisher

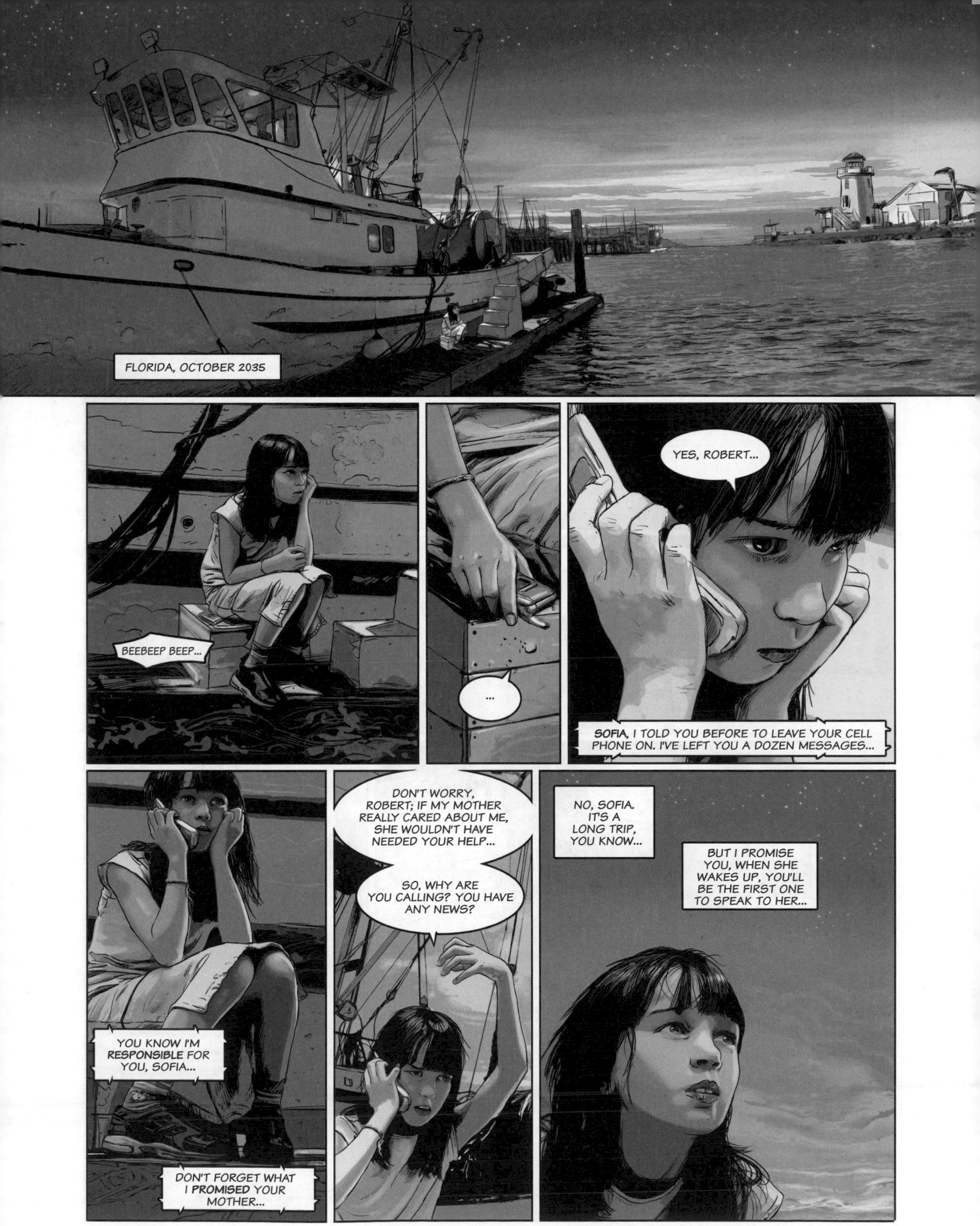
FLORIDA, OCTOBER 2035
BEEBEEP BEEP...
...
YES, ROBERT...
SOFIA, I TOLD YOU BEFORE TO LEAVE YOUR CELL PHONE ON. I'VE LEFT YOU A DOZEN MESSAGES...
YOU KNOW I'M RESPONSIBLE FOR YOU, SOFIA...
DON'T FORGET WHAT I PROMISED YOUR MOTHER...
DON'T WORRY, ROBERT; IF MY MOTHER REALLY CARED ABOUT ME, SHE WOULDN'T HAVE NEEDED YOUR HELP...
SO, WHY ARE YOU CALLING? YOU HAVE ANY NEWS?
NO, SOFIA. IT'S A LONG TRIP, YOU KNOW...
BUT I PROMISE YOU, WHEN SHE WAKES UP, YOU'LL BE THE FIRST ONE TO SPEAK TO HER...

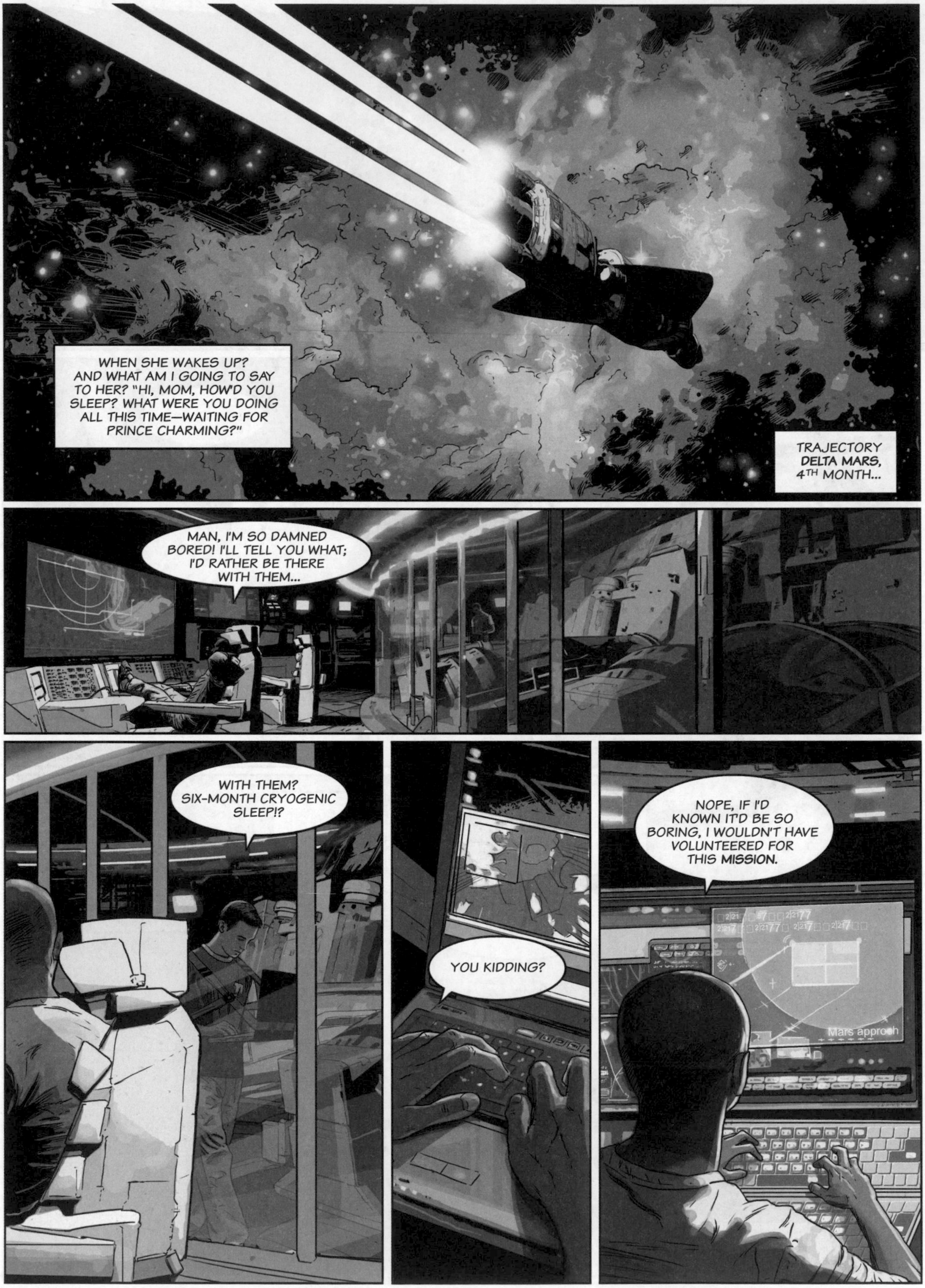
WHEN SHE WAKES UP? AND WHAT AM I GOING TO SAY TO HER? "HI, MOM, HOW'D YOU SLEEP? WHAT WERE YOU DOING ALL THIS TIME—WAITING FOR PRINCE CHARMING?"
TRAJECTORY DELTA MARS, 4TH MONTH...
MAN, I'M SO DAMNED BORED! I'LL TELL YOU WHAT; I'D RATHER BE THERE WITH THEM...
WITH THEM? SIX-MONTH CRYOGENIC SLEEP!?
YOU KIDDING?
NOPE, IF I'D KNOWN IT'D BE SO BORING, I WOULDN'T HAVE VOLUNTEERED FOR THIS MISSION.
Mars approch

EVEN BETTER, I HEAR THAT THING REDUCES YOUR LIFE EXPECTANCY BY AT LEAST DOUBLE THE TIME YOU SPEND INSIDE...

YOU GOTTA REALLY WANT IT...

FRANKLY, YOU CAN KEEP IT.

SHIT, WAIT A MINUTE: I THINK I'VE GOT SOMETHING SERIOUS HERE THAT'LL MAKE YOU WISH YOU'D BEEN CRYOGENISED!!!

Solar Radiation Storm
Impact : 25 sec
Isolation chamber automatic
door locking : 20 sec

A SOLAR RADIATION STORM!!!

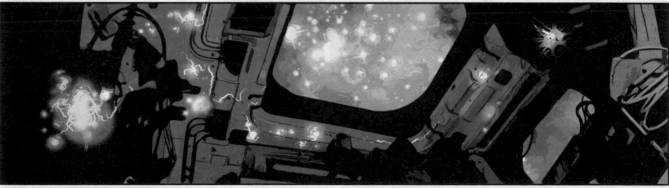

Radioactivity reaching cell destruction limit

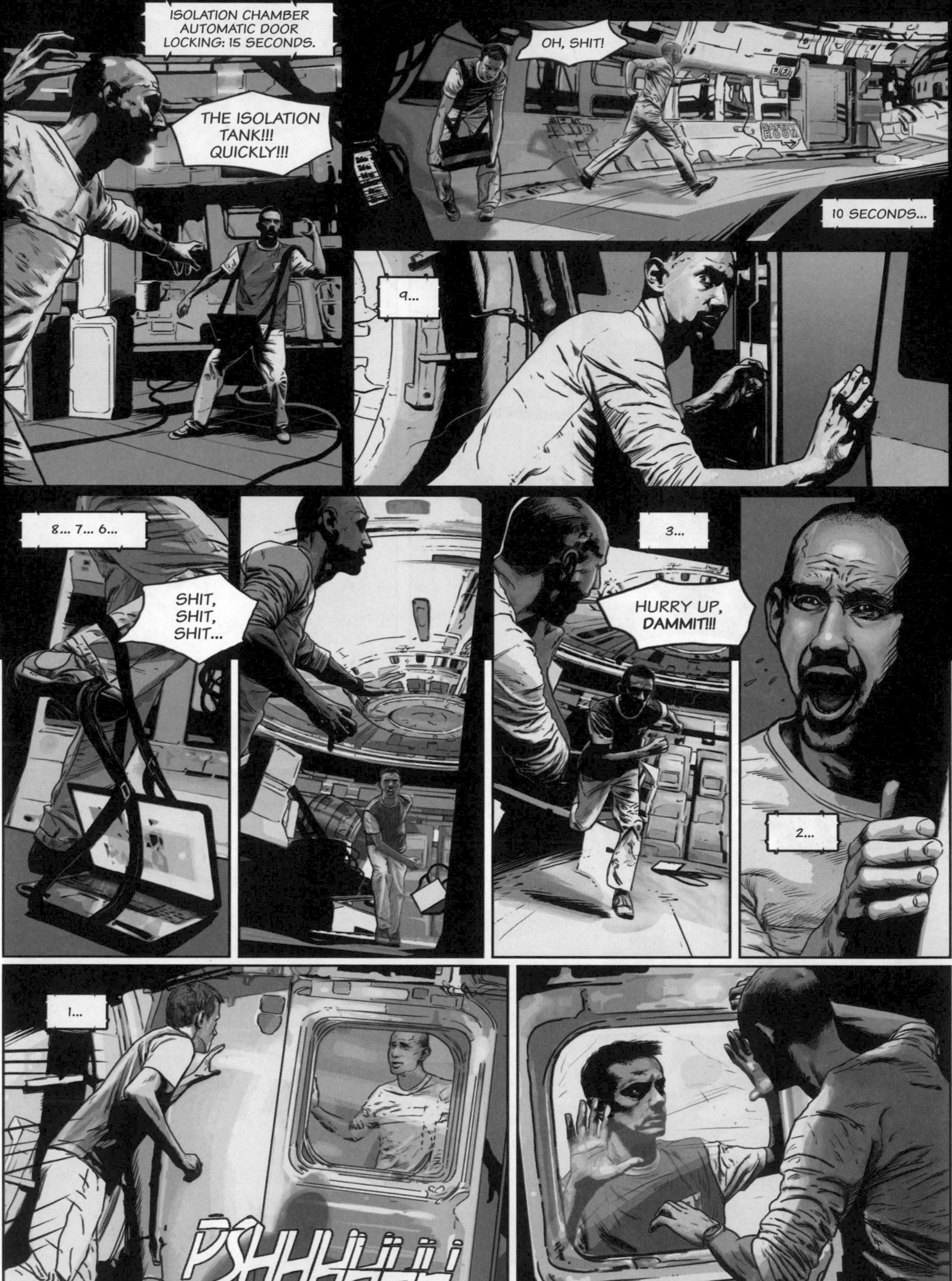
ISOLATION CHAMBER AUTOMATIC DOOR LOCKING: 15 SECONDS.
THE ISOLATION TANK!!! QUICKLY!!!
OH, SHIT!
SAFETY ROOM
10 SECONDS...
9...
8... 7... 6...
SHIT, SHIT, SHIT...
3...
HURRY UP, DAMMIT!!!
2...
1...
PSHHHHHH!

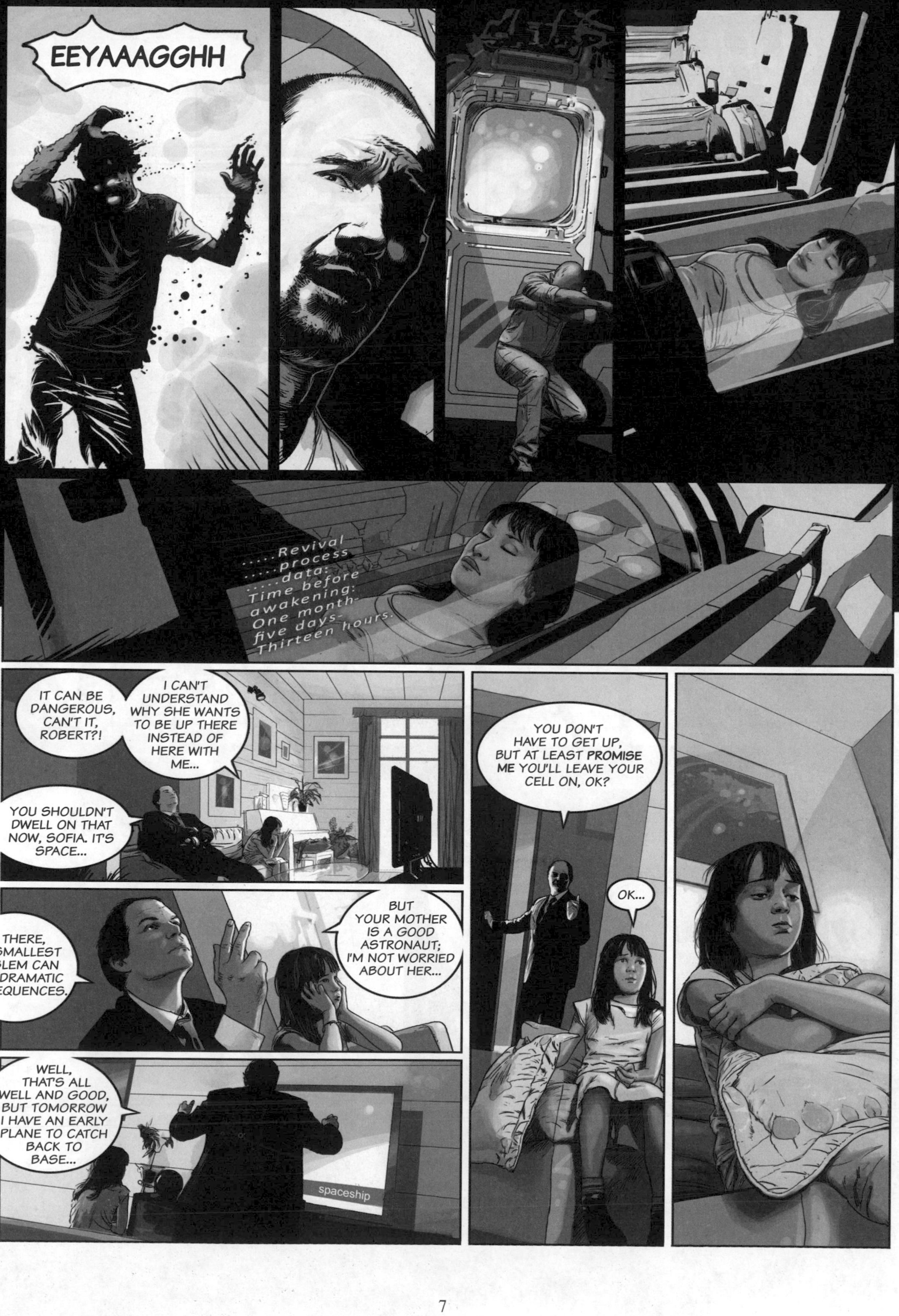
EEYAAAGGHH
.....Revival .....process .....data: Time before awakening: One month- five days- Thirteen hours.
IT CAN BE DANGEROUS, CAN'T IT, ROBERT?!
I CAN'T UNDERSTAND WHY SHE WANTS TO BE UP THERE INSTEAD OF HERE WITH ME...
YOU SHOULDN'T DWELL ON THAT NOW, SOFIA. IT'S SPACE...
UP THERE, THE SMALLEST PROBLEM CAN HAVE DRAMATIC CONSEQUENCES.
BUT YOUR MOTHER IS A GOOD ASTRONAUT; I'M NOT WORRIED ABOUT HER...
WELL, THAT'S ALL WELL AND GOOD, BUT TOMORROW I HAVE AN EARLY PLANE TO CATCH BACK TO BASE...
spaceship
YOU DON'T HAVE TO GET UP, BUT AT LEAST **PROMISE ME** YOU'LL LEAVE YOUR CELL ON, OK?
OK...

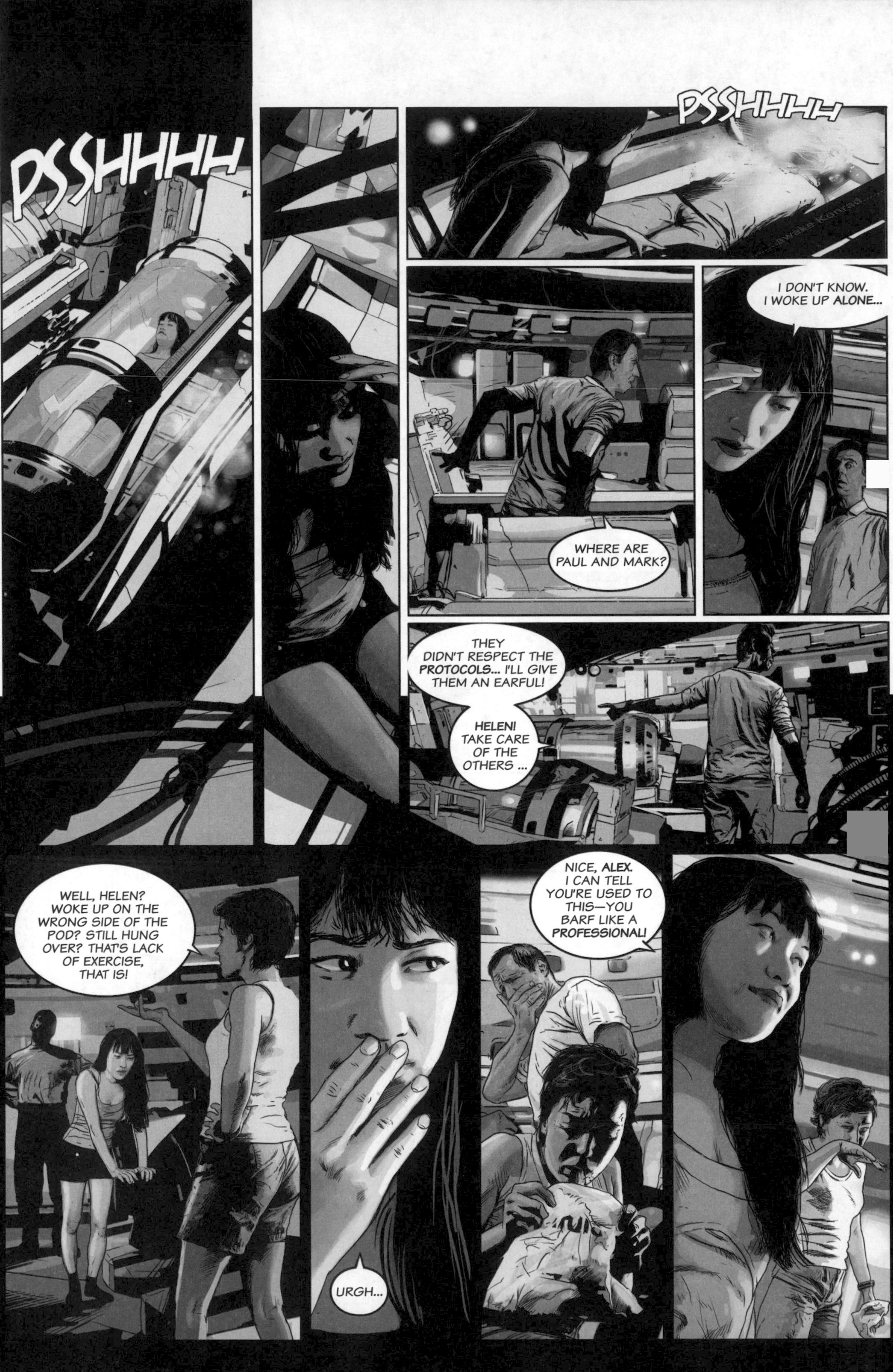
PSSHHHH
PSSHHHH
I DON'T KNOW. I WOKE UP ALONE...
WHERE ARE PAUL AND MARK?
THEY DIDN'T RESPECT THE PROTOCOLS... I'LL GIVE THEM AN EARFUL!
HELEN! TAKE CARE OF THE OTHERS ...
WELL, HELEN? WOKE UP ON THE WRONG SIDE OF THE POD? STILL HUNG OVER? THAT'S LACK OF EXERCISE, THAT IS!
URGH...
NICE, ALEX. I CAN TELL YOU'RE USED TO THIS—YOU BARF LIKE A PROFESSIONAL!

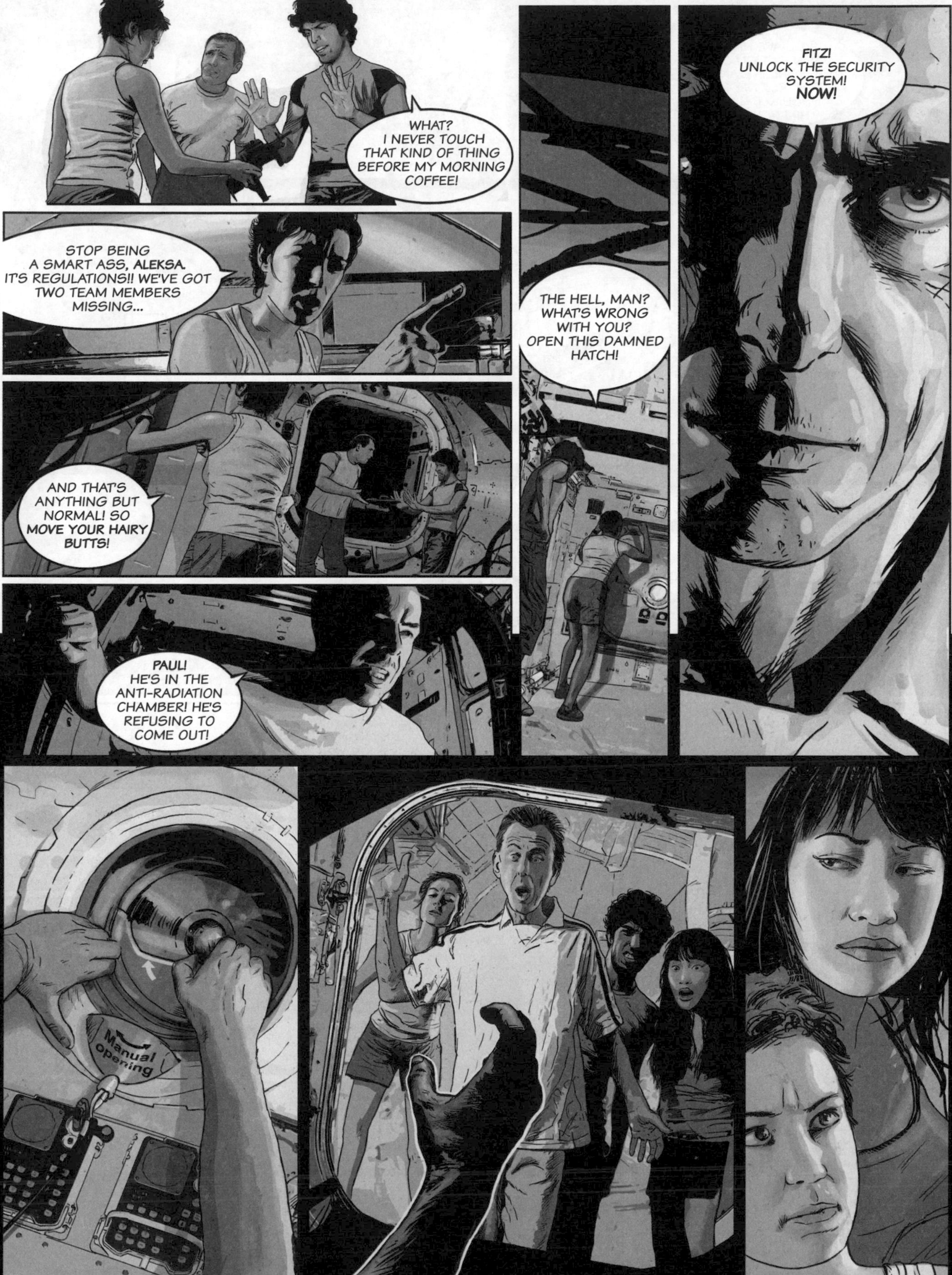
WHAT? I NEVER TOUCH THAT KIND OF THING BEFORE MY MORNING COFFEE!
STOP BEING A SMART ASS, ALEKSA. IT'S REGULATIONS!! WE'VE GOT TWO TEAM MEMBERS MISSING...
AND THAT'S ANYTHING BUT NORMAL! SO MOVE YOUR HAIRY BUTTS!
PAUL! HE'S IN THE ANTI-RADIATION CHAMBER! HE'S REFUSING TO COME OUT!
THE HELL, MAN? WHAT'S WRONG WITH YOU? OPEN THIS DAMNED HATCH!
FITZ! UNLOCK THE SECURITY SYSTEM! NOW!
Manual Opening

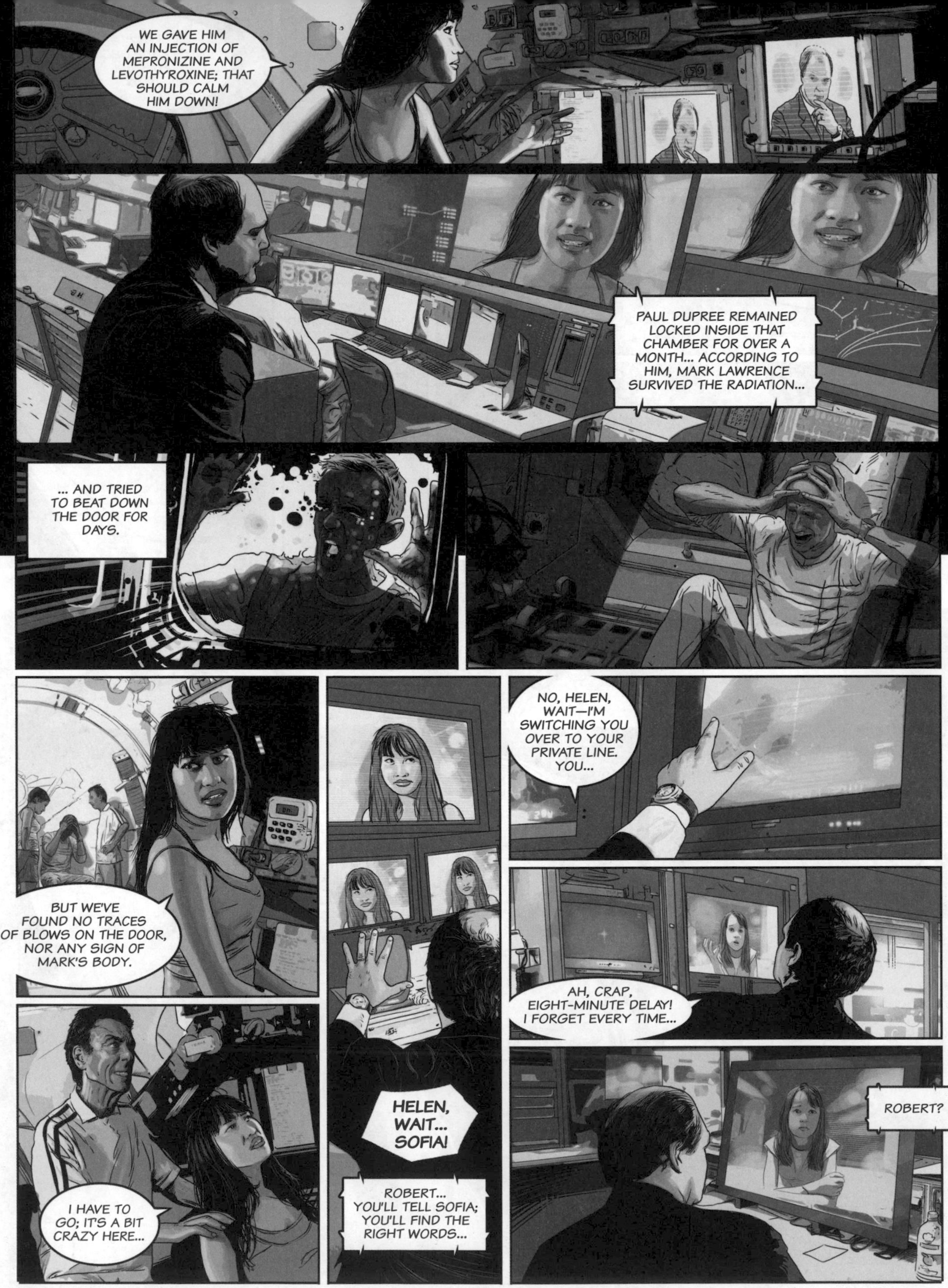
WE GAVE HIM AN INJECTION OF MEPRONIZINE AND LEVOTHYROXINE; THAT SHOULD CALM HIM DOWN!
PAUL DUPREE REMAINED LOCKED INSIDE THAT CHAMBER FOR OVER A MONTH... ACCORDING TO HIM, MARK LAWRENCE SURVIVED THE RADIATION...
... AND TRIED TO BEAT DOWN THE DOOR FOR DAYS.
BUT WE'VE FOUND NO TRACES OF BLOWS ON THE DOOR, NOR ANY SIGN OF MARK'S BODY.
I HAVE TO GO; IT'S A BIT CRAZY HERE...
HELEN, WAIT... SOFIA!
ROBERT... YOU'LL TELL SOFIA; YOU'LL FIND THE RIGHT WORDS...
NO, HELEN, WAIT—I'M SWITCHING YOU OVER TO YOUR PRIVATE LINE. YOU...
AH, CRAP, EIGHT-MINUTE DELAY! I FORGET EVERY TIME...
ROBERT?

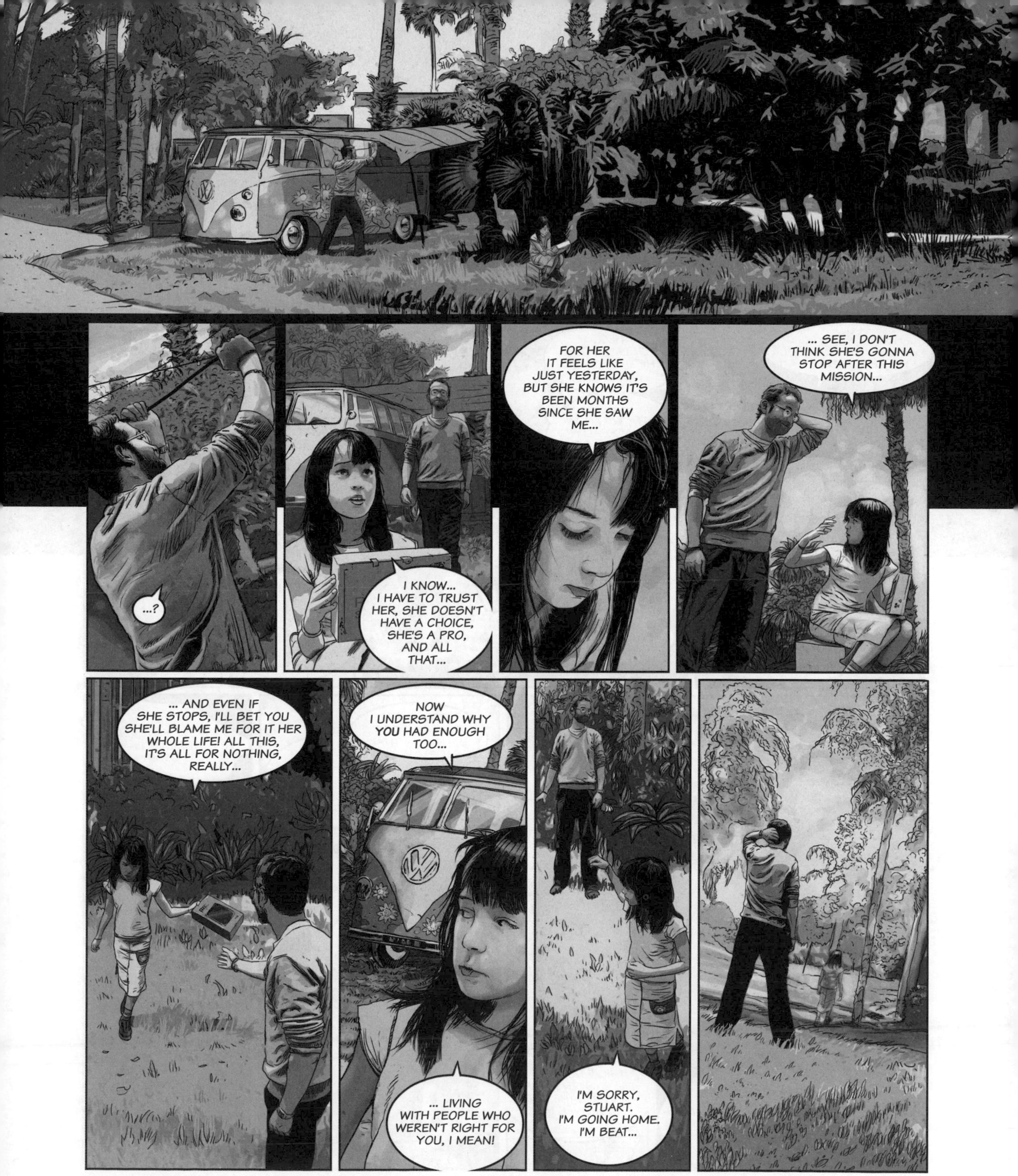
...?
I KNOW... I HAVE TO TRUST HER, SHE DOESN'T HAVE A CHOICE, SHE'S A PRO, AND ALL THAT...
FOR HER IT FEELS LIKE JUST YESTERDAY, BUT SHE KNOWS IT'S BEEN MONTHS SINCE SHE SAW ME...
... SEE, I DON'T THINK SHE'S GONNA STOP AFTER THIS MISSION...
... AND EVEN IF SHE STOPS, I'LL BET YOU SHE'LL BLAME ME FOR IT HER WHOLE LIFE! ALL THIS, IT'S ALL FOR NOTHING, REALLY...
NOW I UNDERSTAND WHY YOU HAD ENOUGH TOO...
... LIVING WITH PEOPLE WHO WEREN'T RIGHT FOR YOU, I MEAN!
I'M SORRY, STUART. I'M GOING HOME. I'M BEAT...

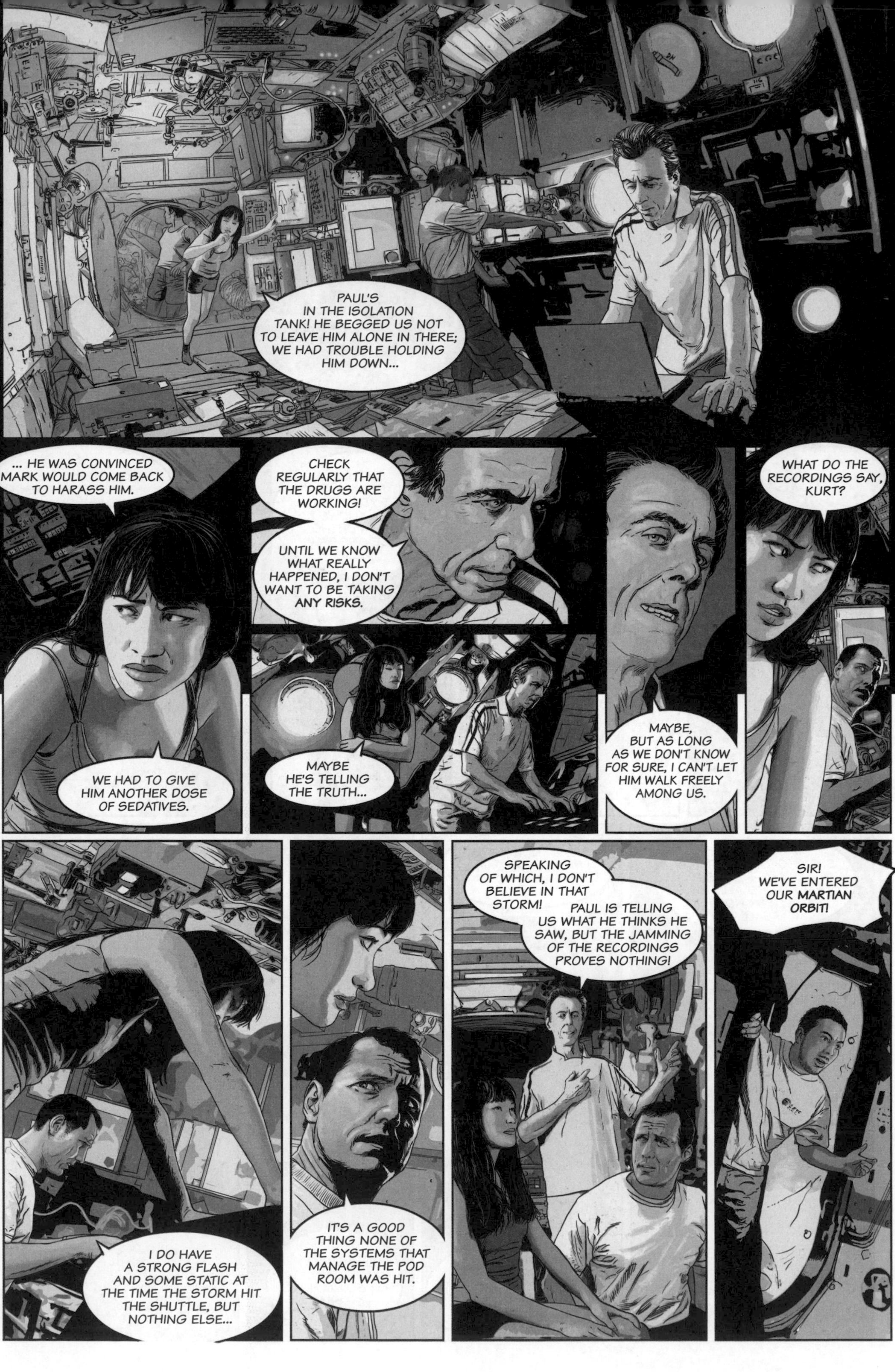
PAUL'S IN THE ISOLATION TANK! HE BEGGED US NOT TO LEAVE HIM ALONE IN THERE; WE HAD TROUBLE HOLDING HIM DOWN...
... HE WAS CONVINCED MARK WOULD COME BACK TO HARASS HIM.
WE HAD TO GIVE HIM ANOTHER DOSE OF SEDATIVES.
CHECK REGULARLY THAT THE DRUGS ARE WORKING!
UNTIL WE KNOW WHAT REALLY HAPPENED, I DON'T WANT TO BE TAKING ANY RISKS.
MAYBE HE'S TELLING THE TRUTH...
MAYBE, BUT AS LONG AS WE DON'T KNOW FOR SURE, I CAN'T LET HIM WALK FREELY AMONG US.
WHAT DO THE RECORDINGS SAY, KURT?
I DO HAVE A STRONG FLASH AND SOME STATIC AT THE TIME THE STORM HIT THE SHUTTLE, BUT NOTHING ELSE...
IT'S A GOOD THING NONE OF THE SYSTEMS THAT MANAGE THE POD ROOM WAS HIT.
SPEAKING OF WHICH, I DON'T BELIEVE IN THAT STORM!
PAUL IS TELLING US WHAT HE THINKS HE SAW, BUT THE JAMMING OF THE RECORDINGS PROVES NOTHING!
SIR! WE'VE ENTERED OUR MARTIAN ORBIT!

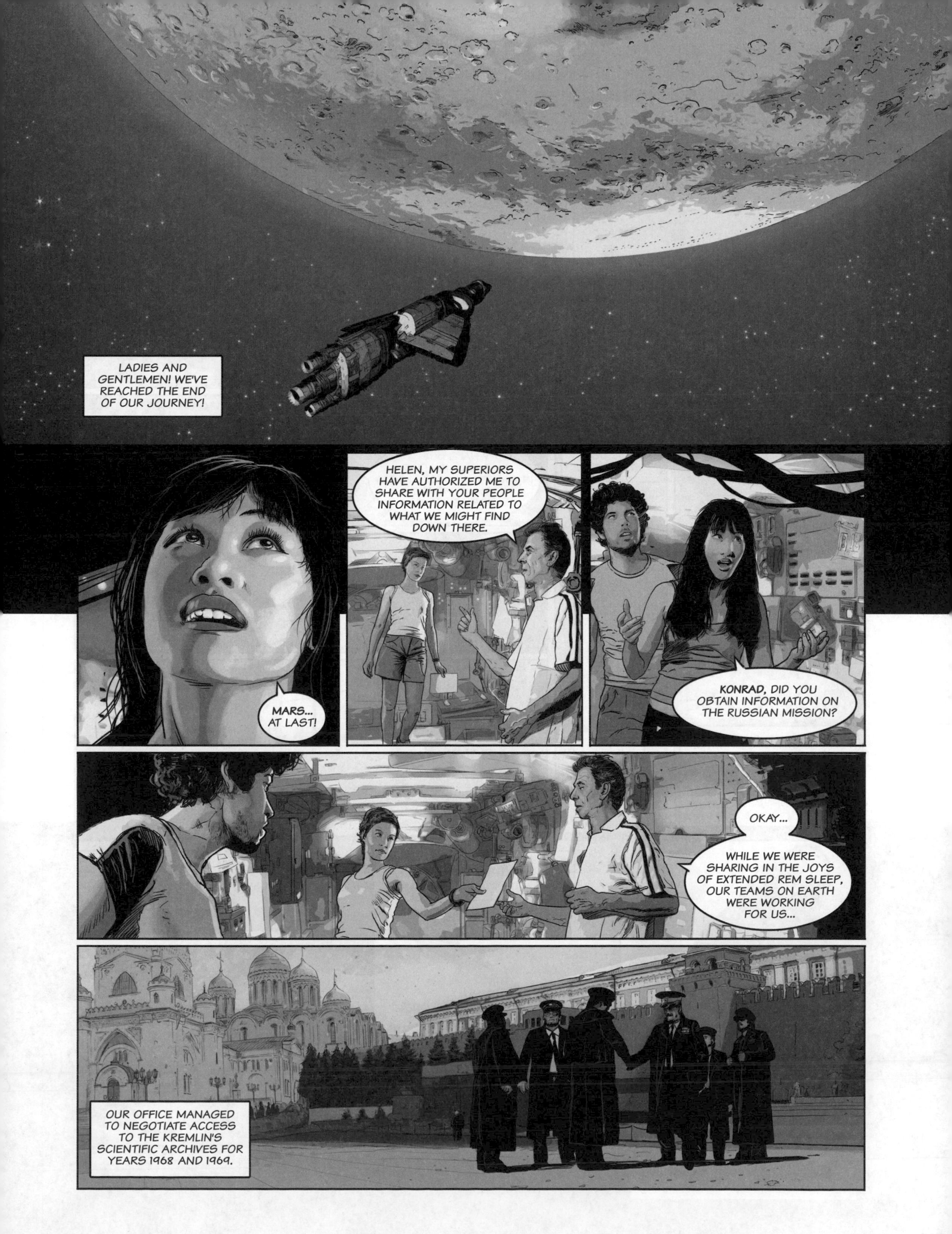
LADIES AND GENTLEMEN! WE'VE REACHED THE END OF OUR JOURNEY!
MARS... AT LAST!
HELEN, MY SUPERIORS HAVE AUTHORIZED ME TO SHARE WITH YOUR PEOPLE INFORMATION RELATED TO WHAT WE MIGHT FIND DOWN THERE.
KONRAD, DID YOU OBTAIN INFORMATION ON THE RUSSIAN MISSION?
OKAY...
WHILE WE WERE SHARING IN THE JOYS OF EXTENDED REM SLEEP, OUR TEAMS ON EARTH WERE WORKING FOR US...
OUR OFFICE MANAGED TO NEGOTIATE ACCESS TO THE KREMLIN'S SCIENTIFIC ARCHIVES FOR YEARS 1968 AND 1969.

WE KNOW THAT THE RUSSIANS WERE FOLLOWING EVERY STEP OF OUR LUNAR PROGRAM, AND WE THOUGHT THEY WERE WORKING ON A SIMILAR PROGRAM...

... BUT THEIR MISSION WAS MORE AMBITIOUS BY FAR.

KHRUSHCHEV AND KOROLEV LAUNCHED THE PROJECT IN 1963...

BUT THE OUSTING OF KHRUSHCHEV THE NEXT YEAR SLOWED THE PROGRAM, AND KOROLEV DIED BEFORE HE COULD SEE THE PROJECT OF HIS CAREER COMPLETED...

THEY CHOSE THE MASTER OF ZVYOZDNY GORODOK, STAR CITY...

YURI GAGARIN!

TO LEAD THE MISSION, THE NEW SOVIET LEADERSHIP NEEDED A COMPETENT MAN, BUT ALSO A HERO WHO WOULD GIVE THEM THE IDEAL FACE OF VICTORY...

WHAT?! BUT YURI GAGARIN DIED IN THE CRASH OF HIS MIG-15 IN 1968!!! EVERYONE KNOWS THAT!

THAT'S WHAT WE ALWAYS BELIEVED.

THE HEADS OF THE PARTY THOUGHT THAT A LEGEND LIKE GAGARIN WOULD BE PERFECT TO APPEASE THE TENSIONS WITHIN THE TEAM.

BUT GAGARIN COULD NOT HAVE DIRECTED THIS MISSION WITHOUT ATTRACTING THE ATTENTION OF OUR SERVICES...

EVERYONE THOUGHT HE WAS IN THE MIG-15 THAT DAY.

EVERYONE BELIEVED IN THE DEATH OF THAT SPACE EXPLORATION HERO.

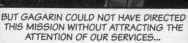

DESPITE THE ARCHAIC NATURE OF TECHNOLOGY AT THE TIME, THE MARTIAN MISSION WENT SMOOTHLY FOR THE FIRST FEW MONTHS.

WHILE THE ENTIRE WORLD WAS WATCHING APOLLO XI'S MOON LANDING, THE RUSSIANS WERE ON THEIR WAY TO MARS...

THEY THOUGHT THEY'D SOON BE ABLE TO SHOW THE WORLD IMAGES OF THIS UNPRECEDENTED SUCCESS.

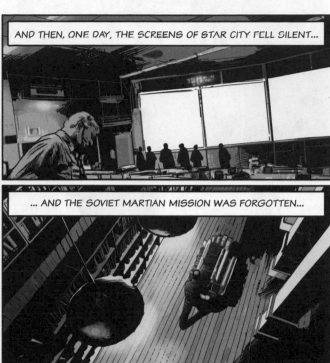

AND THEN, ONE DAY, THE SCREENS OF STAR CITY FELL SILENT...

... AND THE SOVIET MARTIAN MISSION WAS FORGOTTEN...

... UNTIL WE DISCOVERED THE MESSAGE RECORDED BY MICHAEL COLLINS IN THE APOLLO MODULE!

GAGARIN DIDN'T DIE IN THE CRASH OF HIS AIRPLANE IN 1968. HE PROBABLY DIED TWO YEARS LATER ON MARS...

IT'S UP TO US TO DISCOVER WHY, AND HOW IT COULD BE LINKED TO THE RETURN OF OUR TWO DOUBLES...

BAH! WHAT DOES IT MATTER WHERE HE IS AND THE DATE OF HIS DEATH? HE DIED EVENTUALLY...

... AND IT WAS LONG AGO ENOUGH THAT NOBODY GIVES A DAMN.

IF THE RUSSIAN MISSION ALSO SUFFERED UNEXPLAINED PHENOMENA, ALEKSA, THEN YES, IT COULD MATTER...

... BECAUSE THE THREAT WE ARE FACING TODAY MAY NOT BE A SIMPLE CONSEQUENCE OF COLD WAR RIVALRIES.

IT'S DOWN THERE THAT WE SHOULD FIND THE ANSWERS TO OUR QUESTIONS...

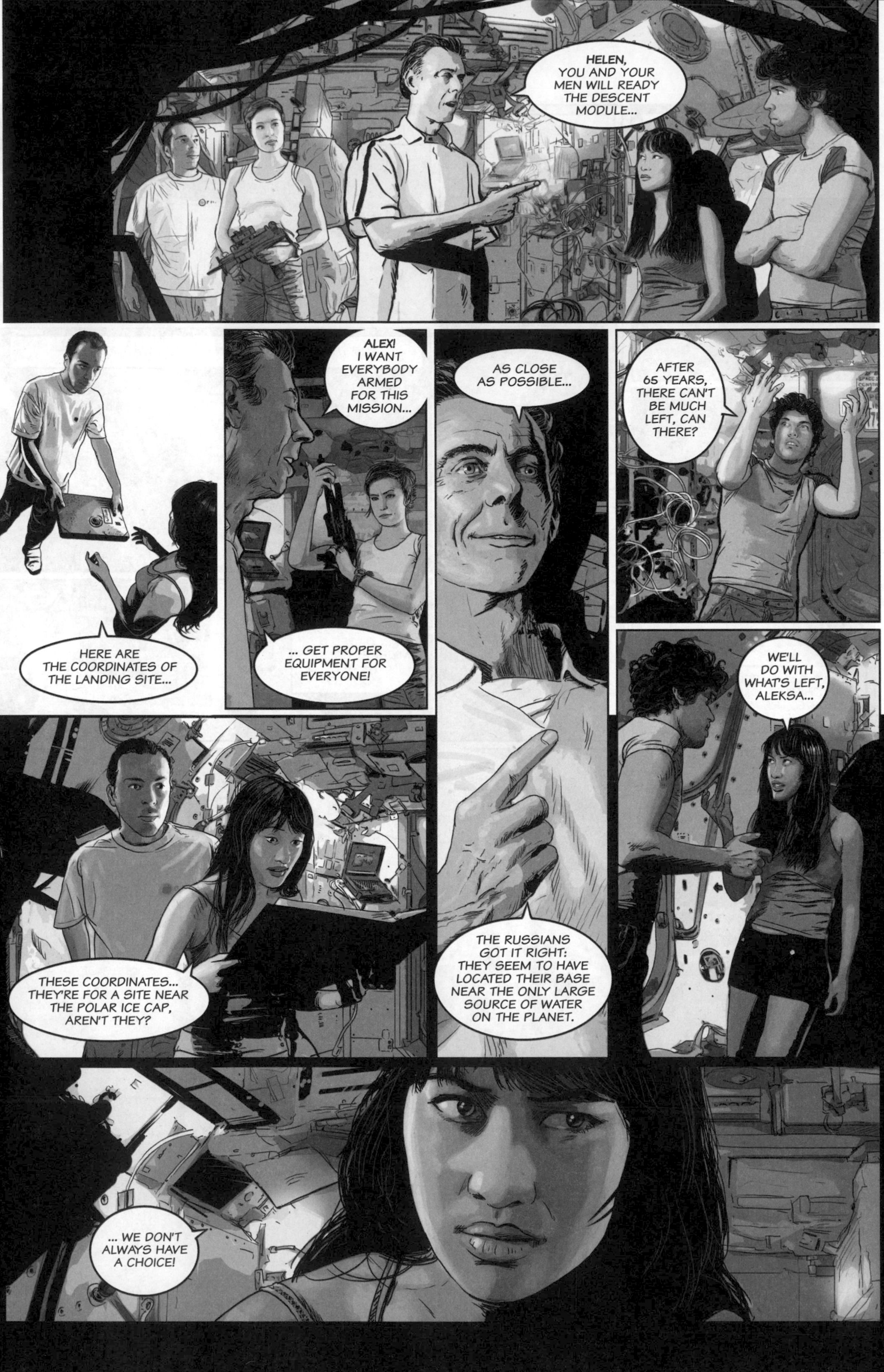
HELEN, YOU AND YOUR MEN WILL READY THE DESCENT MODULE...
HERE ARE THE COORDINATES OF THE LANDING SITE...
ALEX! I WANT EVERYBODY ARMED FOR THIS MISSION...
... GET PROPER EQUIPMENT FOR EVERYONE!
AS CLOSE AS POSSIBLE...
AFTER 65 YEARS, THERE CAN'T BE MUCH LEFT, CAN THERE?
WE'LL DO WITH WHAT'S LEFT, ALEKSA...
THESE COORDINATES... THEY'RE FOR A SITE NEAR THE POLAR ICE CAP, AREN'T THEY?
THE RUSSIANS GOT IT RIGHT: THEY SEEM TO HAVE LOCATED THEIR BASE NEAR THE ONLY LARGE SOURCE OF WATER ON THE PLANET.
... WE DON'T ALWAYS HAVE A CHOICE!

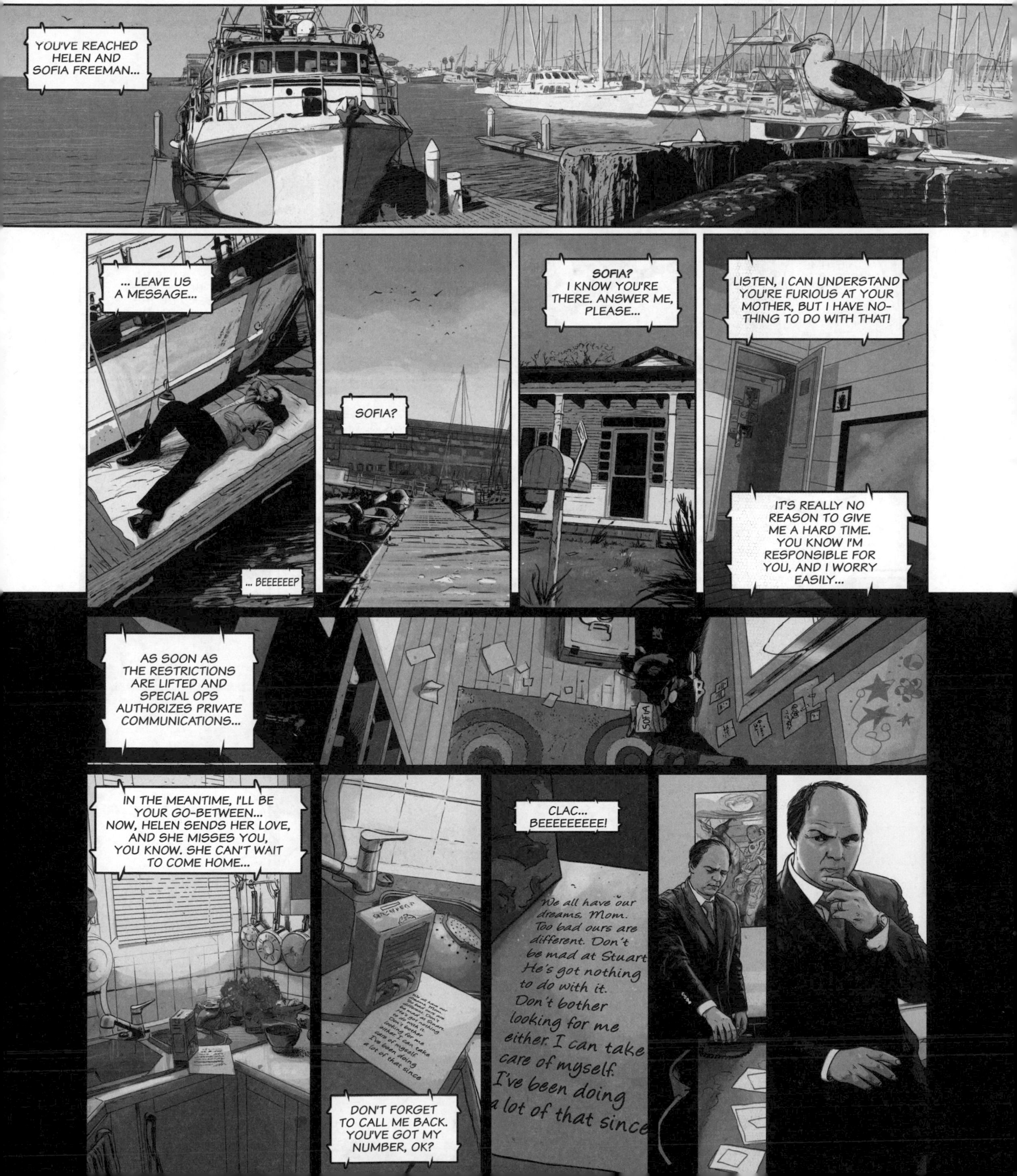
YOU'VE REACHED HELEN AND SOFIA FREEMAN...
... LEAVE US A MESSAGE...
... BEEEEEEP
SOFIA?
SOFIA? I KNOW YOU'RE THERE. ANSWER ME, PLEASE...
LISTEN, I CAN UNDERSTAND YOU'RE FURIOUS AT YOUR MOTHER, BUT I HAVE NO-THING TO DO WITH THAT!
IT'S REALLY NO REASON TO GIVE ME A HARD TIME. YOU KNOW I'M RESPONSIBLE FOR YOU, AND I WORRY EASILY...
AS SOON AS THE RESTRICTIONS ARE LIFTED AND SPECIAL OPS AUTHORIZES PRIVATE COMMUNICATIONS...
IN THE MEANTIME, I'LL BE YOUR GO-BETWEEN... NOW, HELEN SENDS HER LOVE, AND SHE MISSES YOU, YOU KNOW. SHE CAN'T WAIT TO COME HOME...
DON'T FORGET TO CALL ME BACK. YOU'VE GOT MY NUMBER, OK?
CLAC... BEEEEEEEEE!
We all have our dreams, Mom. Too bad ours are different. Don't be mad at Stuart. He's got nothing to do with it. Don't bother looking for me either. I can take care of myself. I've been doing a lot of that since

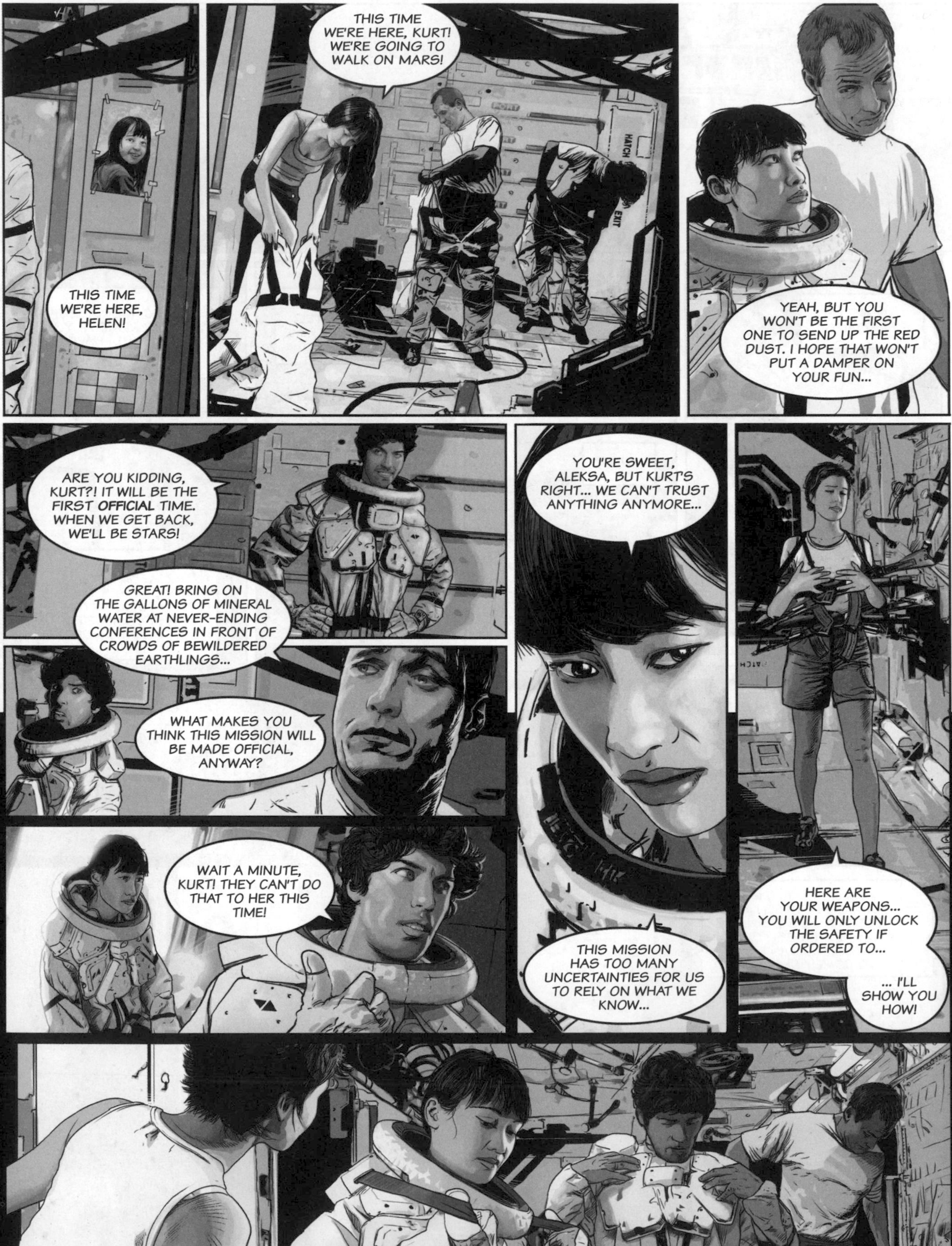
THIS TIME WE'RE HERE, KURT! WE'RE GOING TO WALK ON MARS!
THIS TIME WE'RE HERE, HELEN!
YEAH, BUT YOU WON'T BE THE FIRST ONE TO SEND UP THE RED DUST. I HOPE THAT WON'T PUT A DAMPER ON YOUR FUN...
ARE YOU KIDDING, KURT?! IT WILL BE THE FIRST OFFICIAL TIME. WHEN WE GET BACK, WE'LL BE STARS!
GREAT! BRING ON THE GALLONS OF MINERAL WATER AT NEVER-ENDING CONFERENCES IN FRONT OF CROWDS OF BEWILDERED EARTHLINGS...
WHAT MAKES YOU THINK THIS MISSION WILL BE MADE OFFICIAL, ANYWAY?
WAIT A MINUTE, KURT! THEY CAN'T DO THAT TO HER THIS TIME!
YOU'RE SWEET, ALEKSA, BUT KURT'S RIGHT... WE CAN'T TRUST ANYTHING ANYMORE...
THIS MISSION HAS TOO MANY UNCERTAINTIES FOR US TO RELY ON WHAT WE KNOW...
HERE ARE YOUR WEAPONS... YOU WILL ONLY UNLOCK THE SAFETY IF ORDERED TO...
... I'LL SHOW YOU HOW!

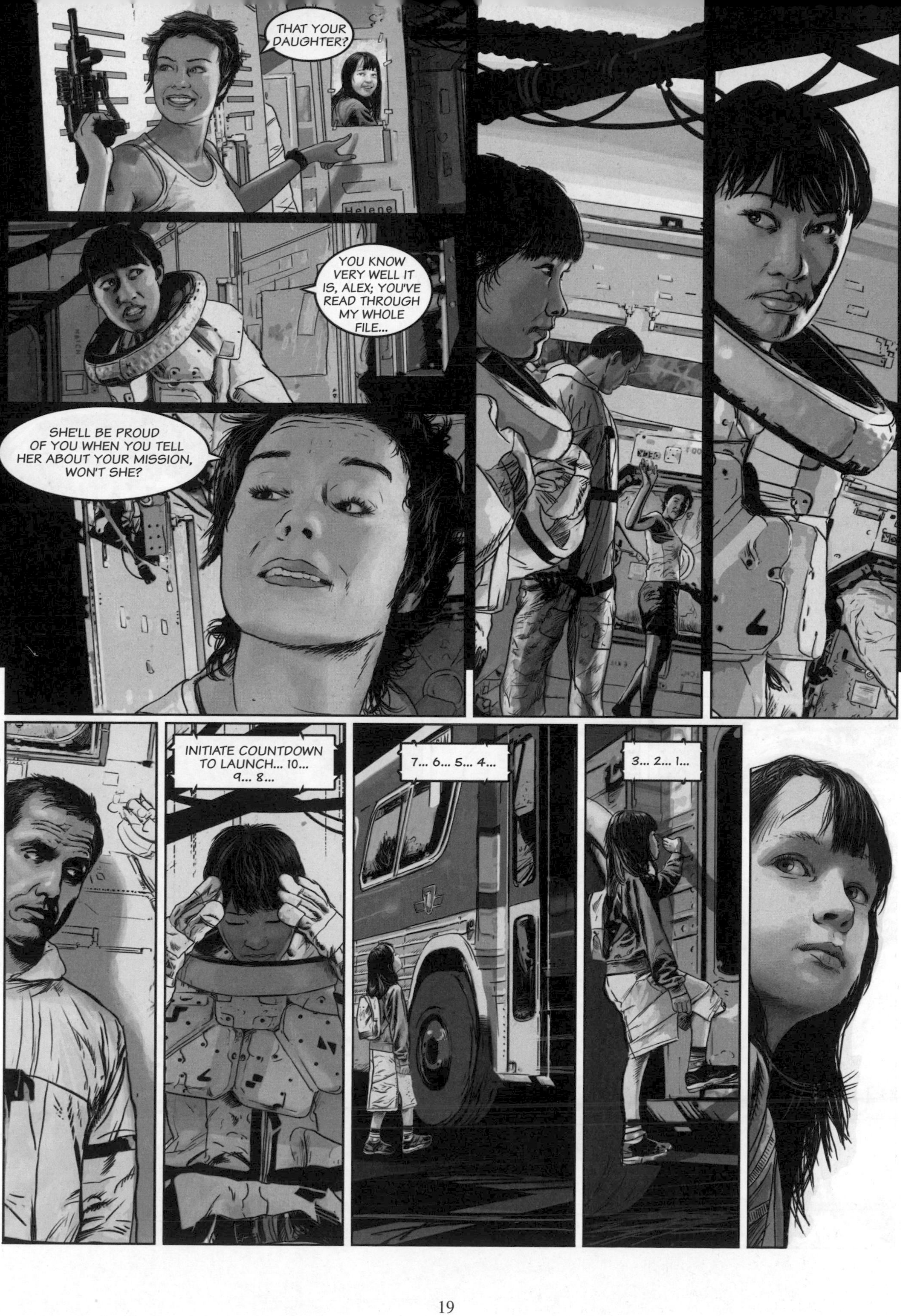

THAT YOUR DAUGHTER?
Helene
YOU KNOW VERY WELL IT IS, ALEX; YOU'VE READ THROUGH MY WHOLE FILE...
SHE'LL BE PROUD OF YOU WHEN YOU TELL HER ABOUT YOUR MISSION, WON'T SHE?
INITIATE COUNTDOWN TO LAUNCH... 10... 9... 8...
7... 6... 5... 4...
3... 2... 1...

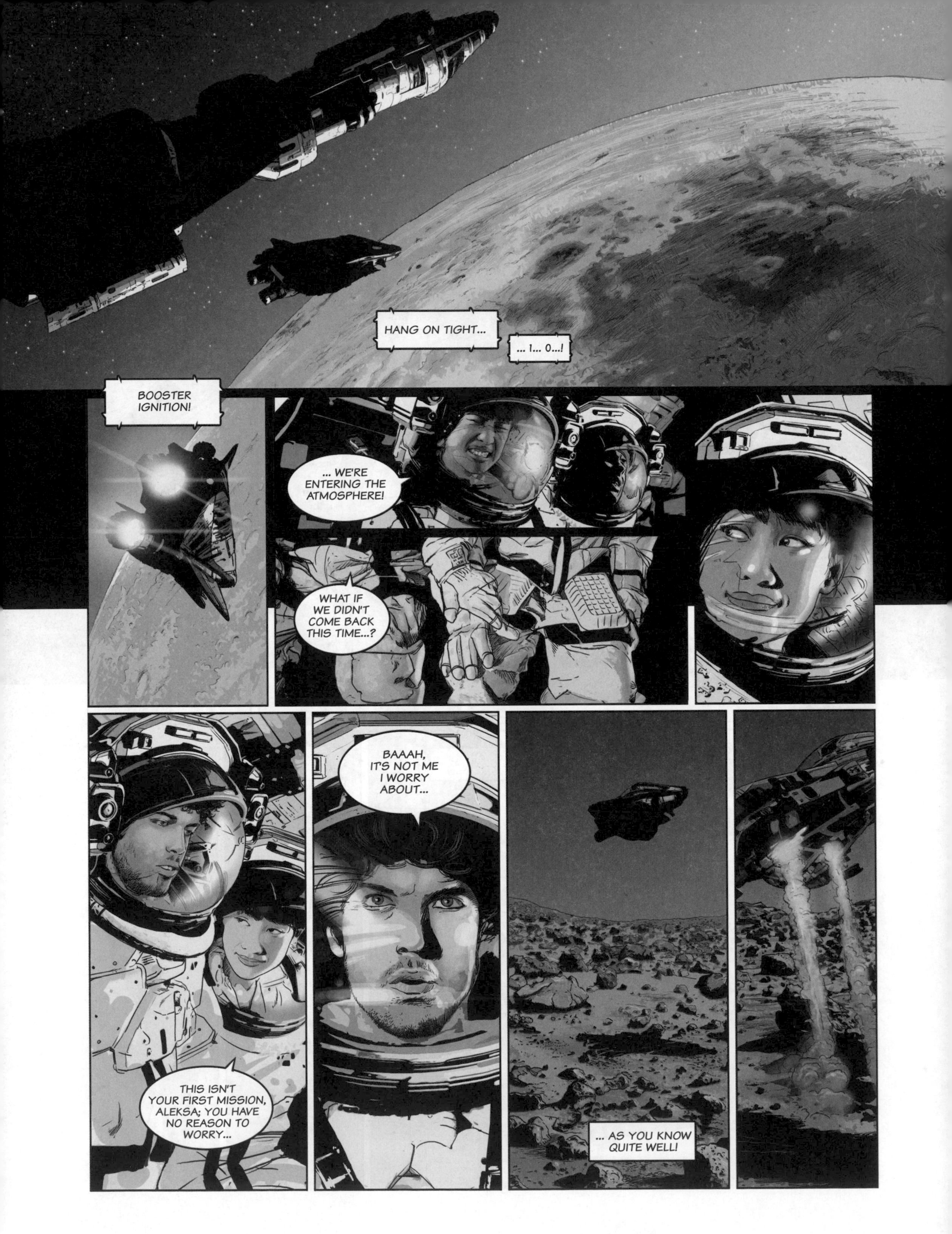
HANG ON TIGHT...
... 1... 0...!
BOOSTER IGNITION!
... WE'RE ENTERING THE ATMOSPHERE!
WHAT IF WE DIDN'T COME BACK THIS TIME...?
THIS ISN'T YOUR FIRST MISSION, ALEKSA; YOU HAVE NO REASON TO WORRY...
BAAAH, IT'S NOT ME I WORRY ABOUT...
... AS YOU KNOW QUITE WELL!

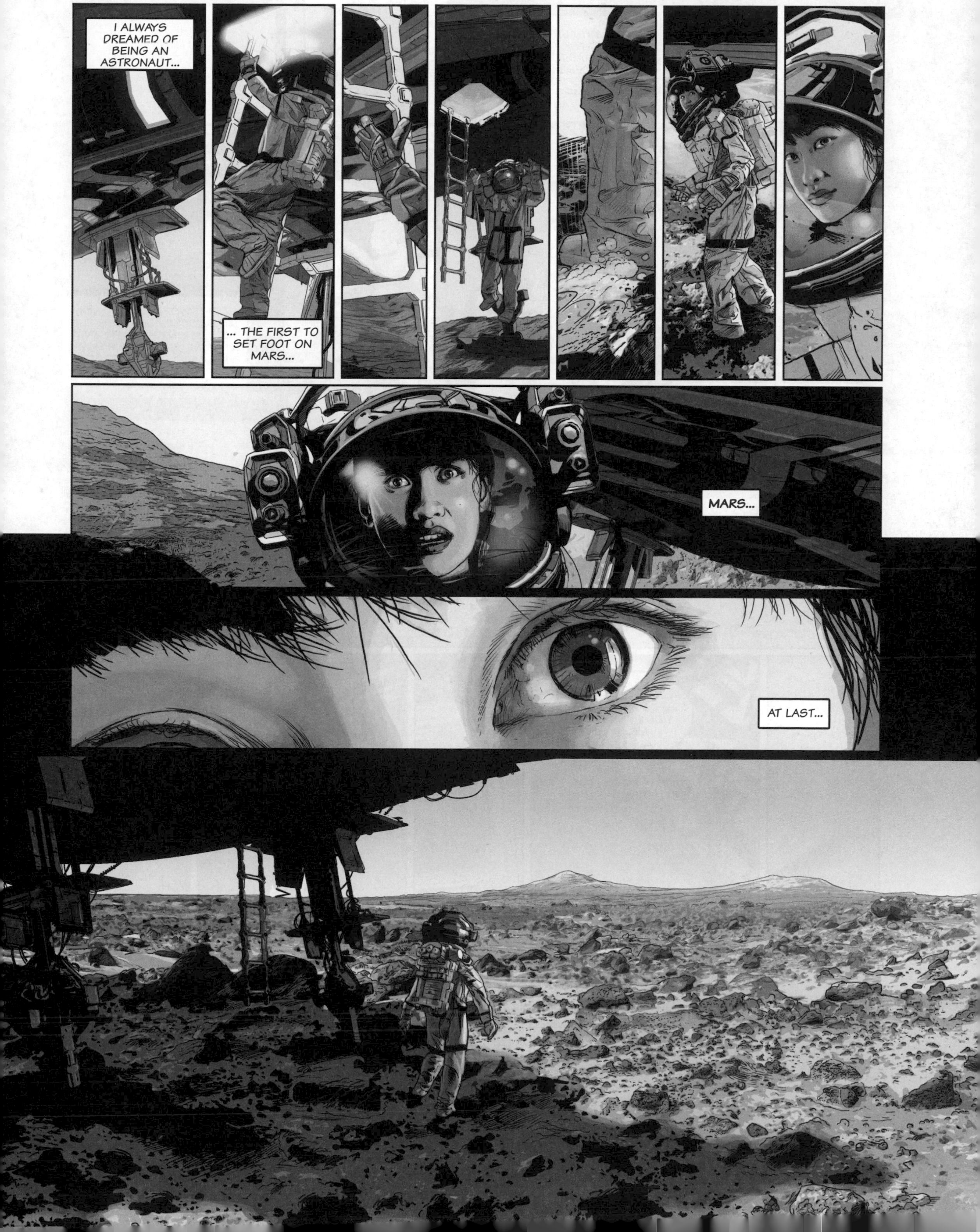
I ALWAYS DREAMED OF BEING AN ASTRONAUT...
... THE FIRST TO SET FOOT ON MARS...
MARS...
AT LAST...

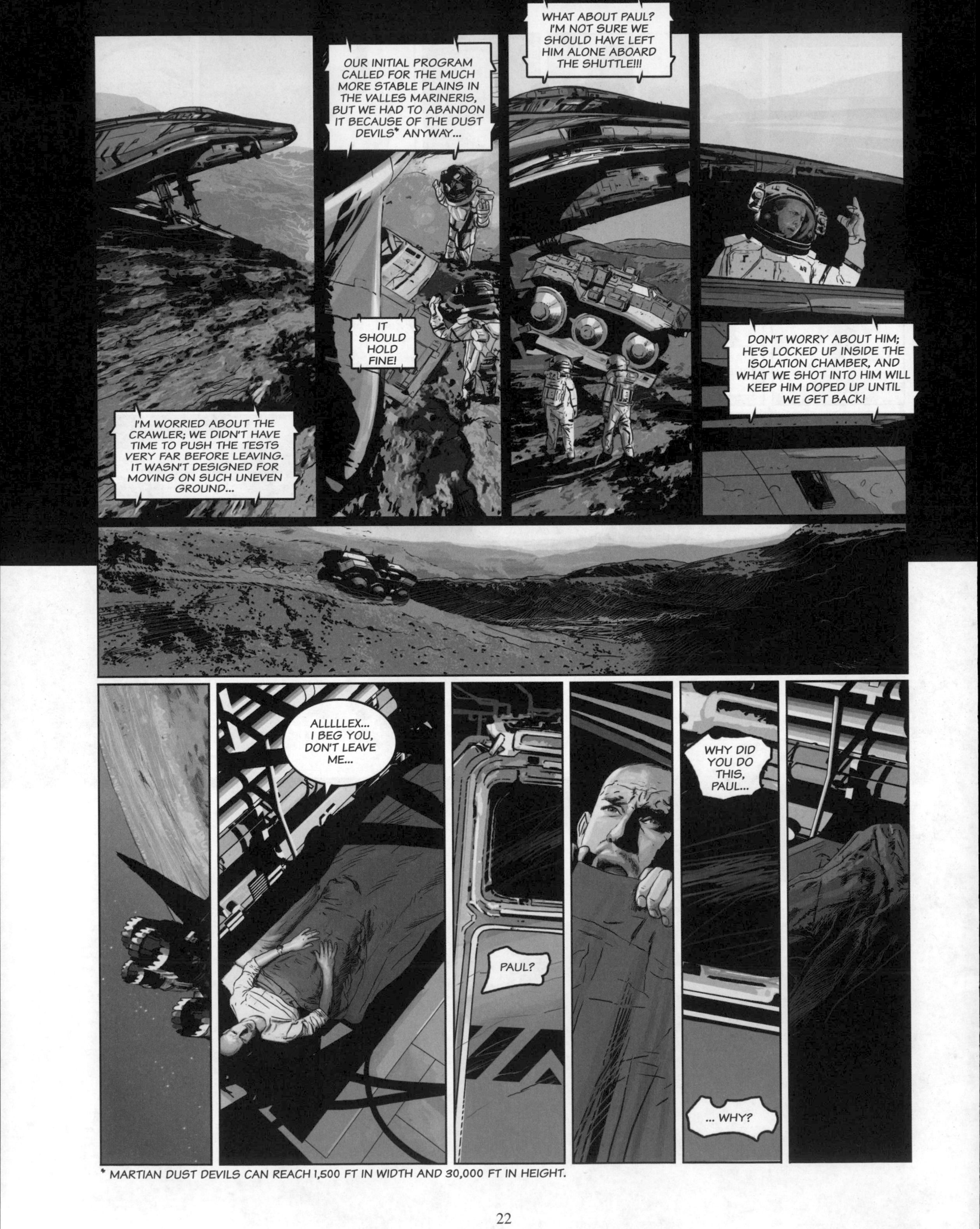
I'M WORRIED ABOUT THE CRAWLER; WE DIDN'T HAVE TIME TO PUSH THE TESTS VERY FAR BEFORE LEAVING. IT WASN'T DESIGNED FOR MOVING ON SUCH UNEVEN GROUND...
OUR INITIAL PROGRAM CALLED FOR THE MUCH MORE STABLE PLAINS IN THE VALLES MARINERIS, BUT WE HAD TO ABANDON IT BECAUSE OF THE DUST DEVILS* ANYWAY...
IT SHOULD HOLD FINE!
WHAT ABOUT PAUL? I'M NOT SURE WE SHOULD HAVE LEFT HIM ALONE ABOARD THE SHUTTLE!!!
DON'T WORRY ABOUT HIM; HE'S LOCKED UP INSIDE THE ISOLATION CHAMBER, AND WHAT WE SHOT INTO HIM WILL KEEP HIM DOPED UP UNTIL WE GET BACK!
ALLLLLEX... I BEG YOU, DON'T LEAVE ME...
PAUL?
WHY DID YOU DO THIS, PAUL...
... WHY?

* MARTIAN DUST DEVILS CAN REACH 1,500 FT IN WIDTH AND 30,000 FT IN HEIGHT.

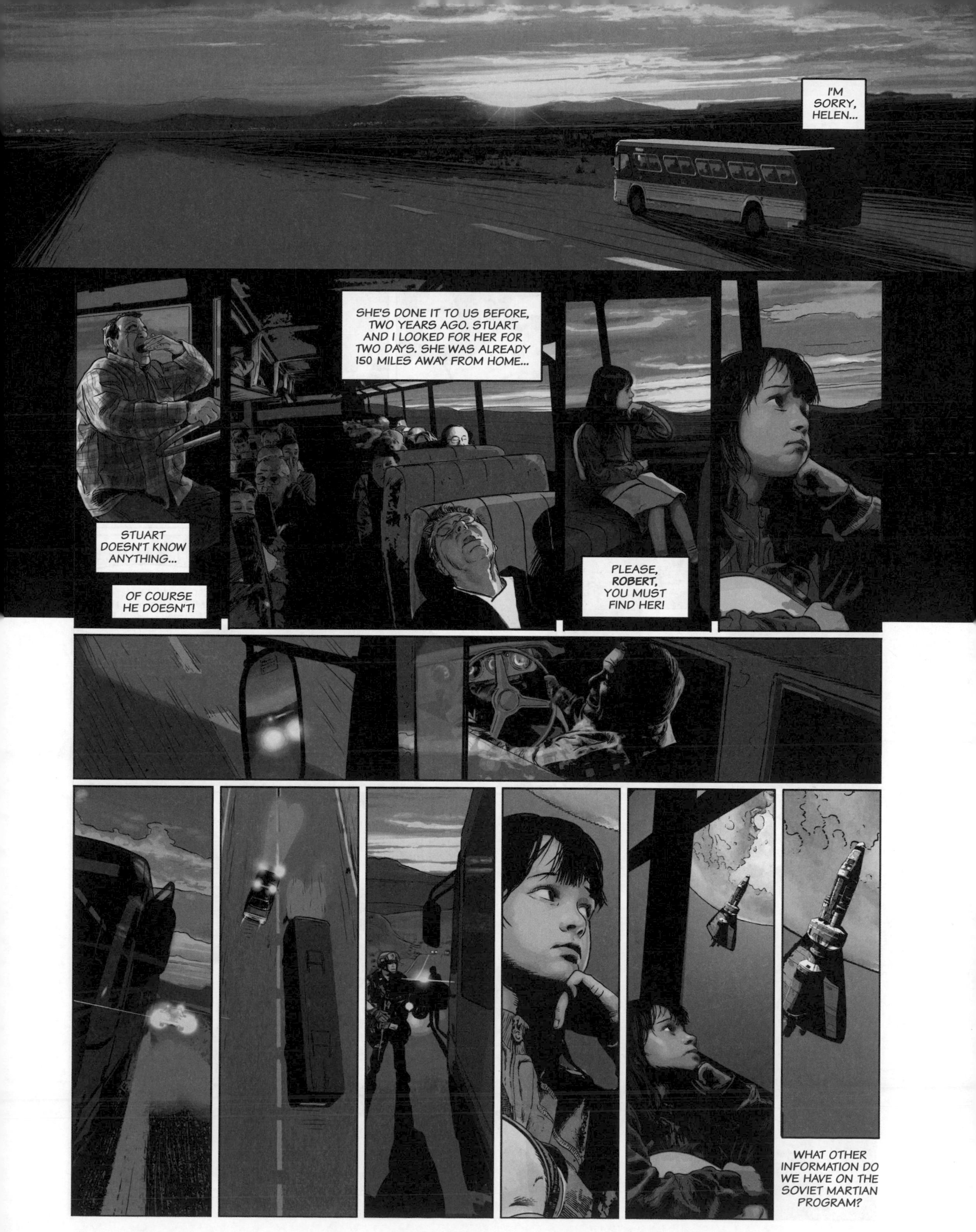
I'M SORRY, HELEN...
STUART DOESN'T KNOW ANYTHING...
OF COURSE HE DOESN'T!
SHE'S DONE IT TO US BEFORE, TWO YEARS AGO. STUART AND I LOOKED FOR HER FOR TWO DAYS. SHE WAS ALREADY 150 MILES AWAY FROM HOME...
PLEASE, ROBERT, YOU MUST FIND HER!
WHAT OTHER INFORMATION DO WE HAVE ON THE SOVIET MARTIAN PROGRAM?

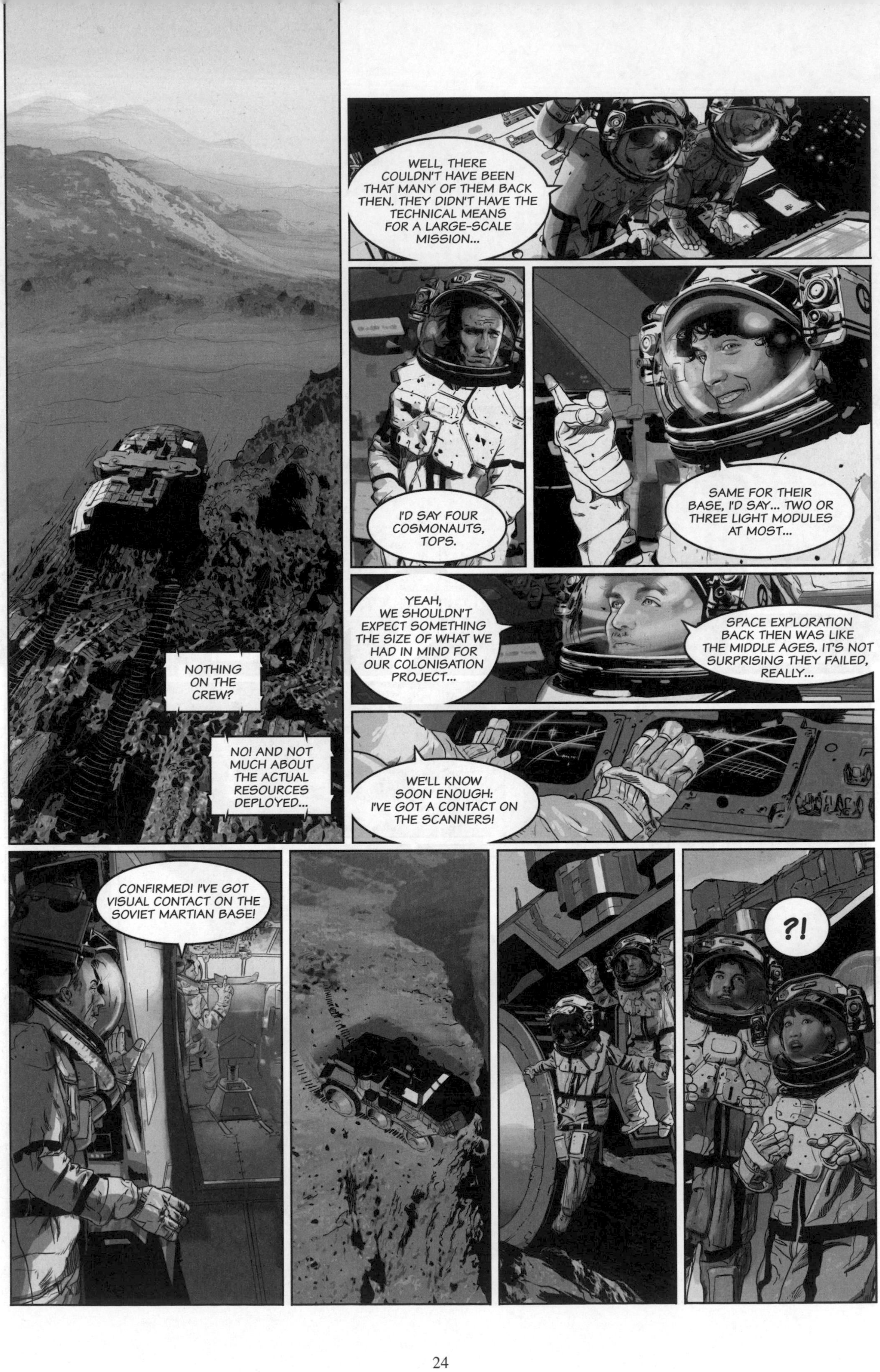
WELL, THERE COULDN'T HAVE BEEN THAT MANY OF THEM BACK THEN. THEY DIDN'T HAVE THE TECHNICAL MEANS FOR A LARGE-SCALE MISSION...
I'D SAY FOUR COSMONAUTS, TOPS.
SAME FOR THEIR BASE, I'D SAY... TWO OR THREE LIGHT MODULES AT MOST...
YEAH, WE SHOULDN'T EXPECT SOMETHING THE SIZE OF WHAT WE HAD IN MIND FOR OUR COLONISATION PROJECT...
SPACE EXPLORATION BACK THEN WAS LIKE THE MIDDLE AGES. IT'S NOT SURPRISING THEY FAILED, REALLY...
NOTHING ON THE CREW?
NO! AND NOT MUCH ABOUT THE ACTUAL RESOURCES DEPLOYED...
WE'LL KNOW SOON ENOUGH: I'VE GOT A CONTACT ON THE SCANNERS!
CONFIRMED! I'VE GOT VISUAL CONTACT ON THE SOVIET MARTIAN BASE!
?!

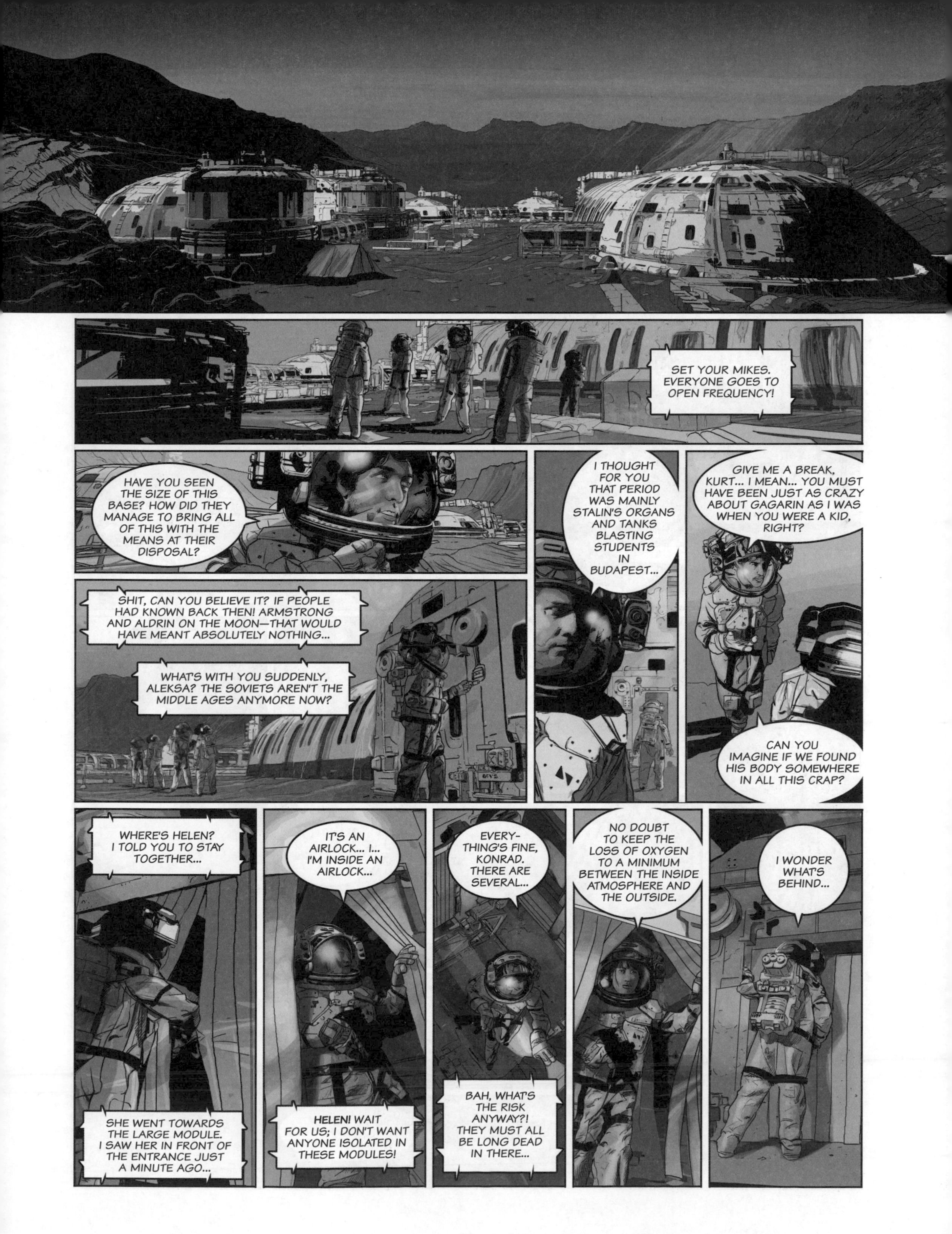

SET YOUR MIKES. EVERYONE GOES TO OPEN FREQUENCY!
HAVE YOU SEEN THE SIZE OF THIS BASE? HOW DID THEY MANAGE TO BRING ALL OF THIS WITH THE MEANS AT THEIR DISPOSAL?
SHIT, CAN YOU BELIEVE IT? IF PEOPLE HAD KNOWN BACK THEN! ARMSTRONG AND ALDRIN ON THE MOON—THAT WOULD HAVE MEANT ABSOLUTELY NOTHING...
WHAT'S WITH YOU SUDDENLY, ALEKSA? THE SOVIETS AREN'T THE MIDDLE AGES ANYMORE NOW?
I THOUGHT FOR YOU THAT PERIOD WAS MAINLY STALIN'S ORGANS AND TANKS BLASTING STUDENTS IN BUDAPEST...
GIVE ME A BREAK, KURT... I MEAN... YOU MUST HAVE BEEN JUST AS CRAZY ABOUT GAGARIN AS I WAS WHEN YOU WERE A KID, RIGHT?
CAN YOU IMAGINE IF WE FOUND HIS BODY SOMEWHERE IN ALL THIS CRAP?
WHERE'S HELEN? I TOLD YOU TO STAY TOGETHER...
SHE WENT TOWARDS THE LARGE MODULE. I SAW HER IN FRONT OF THE ENTRANCE JUST A MINUTE AGO...
IT'S AN AIRLOCK... I... I'M INSIDE AN AIRLOCK...
HELEN! WAIT FOR US; I DON'T WANT ANYONE ISOLATED IN THESE MODULES!
EVERY-THING'S FINE, KONRAD. THERE ARE SEVERAL...
BAH, WHAT'S THE RISK ANYWAY?! THEY MUST ALL BE LONG DEAD IN THERE...
NO DOUBT TO KEEP THE LOSS OF OXYGEN TO A MINIMUM BETWEEN THE INSIDE ATMOSPHERE AND THE OUTSIDE.
I WONDER WHAT'S BEHIND...

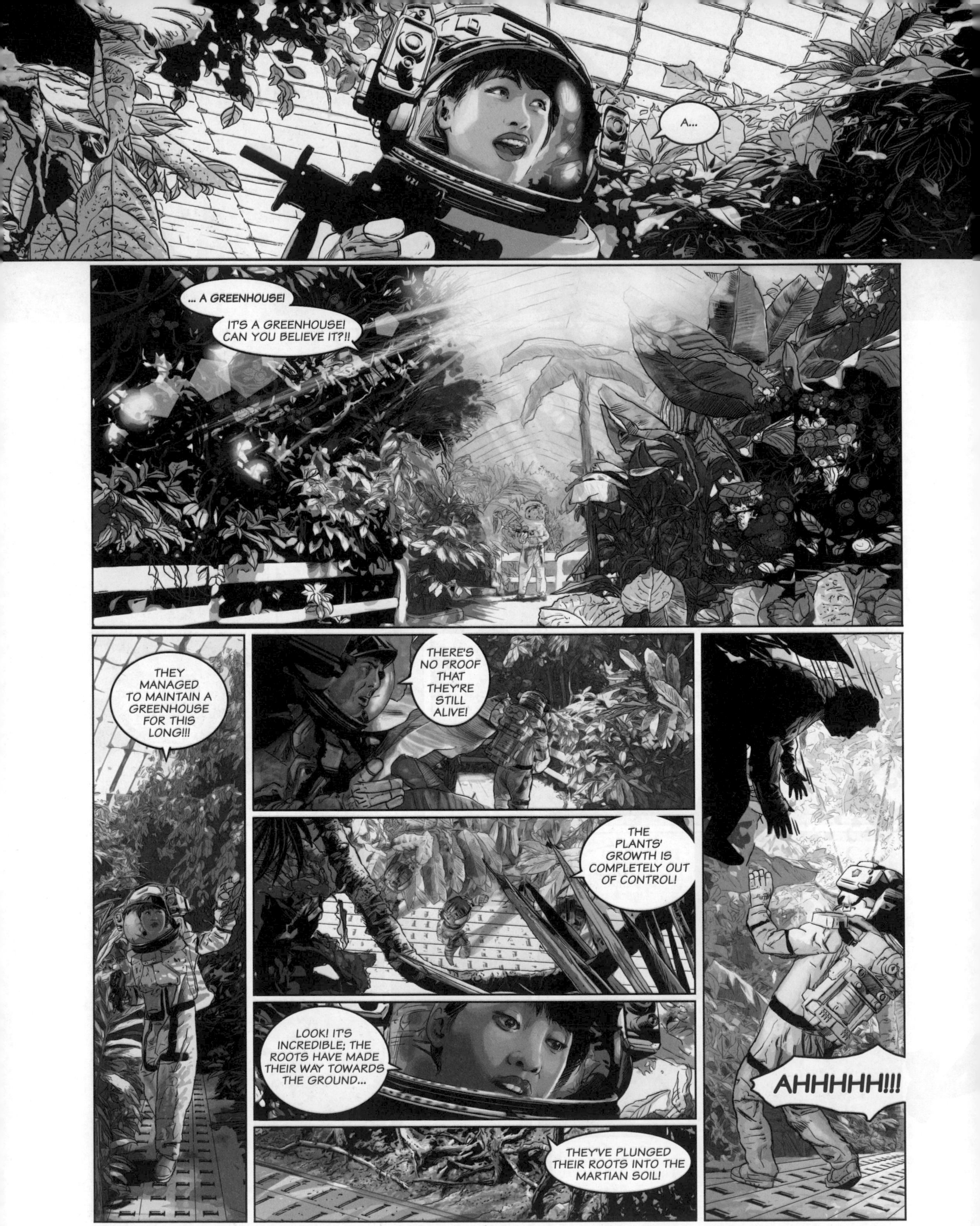
A...
... A GREENHOUSE!
IT'S A GREENHOUSE! CAN YOU BELIEVE IT?!!
THEY MANAGED TO MAINTAIN A GREENHOUSE FOR THIS LONG!!!
THERE'S NO PROOF THAT THEY'RE STILL ALIVE!
THE PLANTS' GROWTH IS COMPLETELY OUT OF CONTROL!
LOOK! IT'S INCREDIBLE; THE ROOTS HAVE MADE THEIR WAY TOWARDS THE GROUND...
THEY'VE PLUNGED THEIR ROOTS INTO THE MARTIAN SOIL!
AHHHHH!!!

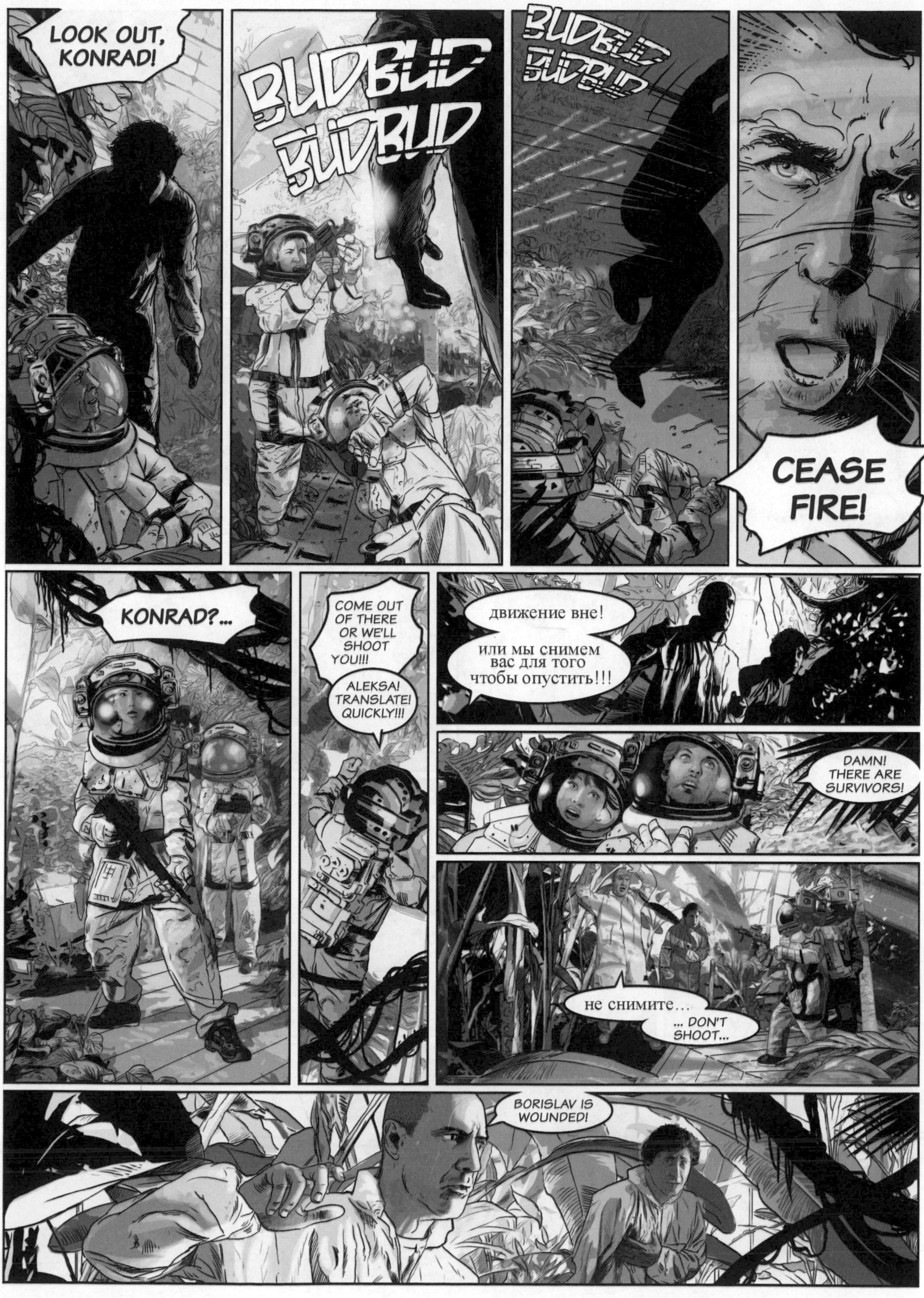
LOOK OUT, KONRAD!
BUDBUD BUDBUD
BUDBUD BUDBUD
CEASE FIRE!
KONRAD?...
COME OUT OF THERE OR WE'LL SHOOT YOU!!!
ALEKSA! TRANSLATE! QUICKLY!!!
движение вне!
или мы снимем вас для того чтобы опустить!!!
DAMN! THERE ARE SURVIVORS!
не снимите…
... DON'T SHOOT...
BORISLAV IS WOUNDED!

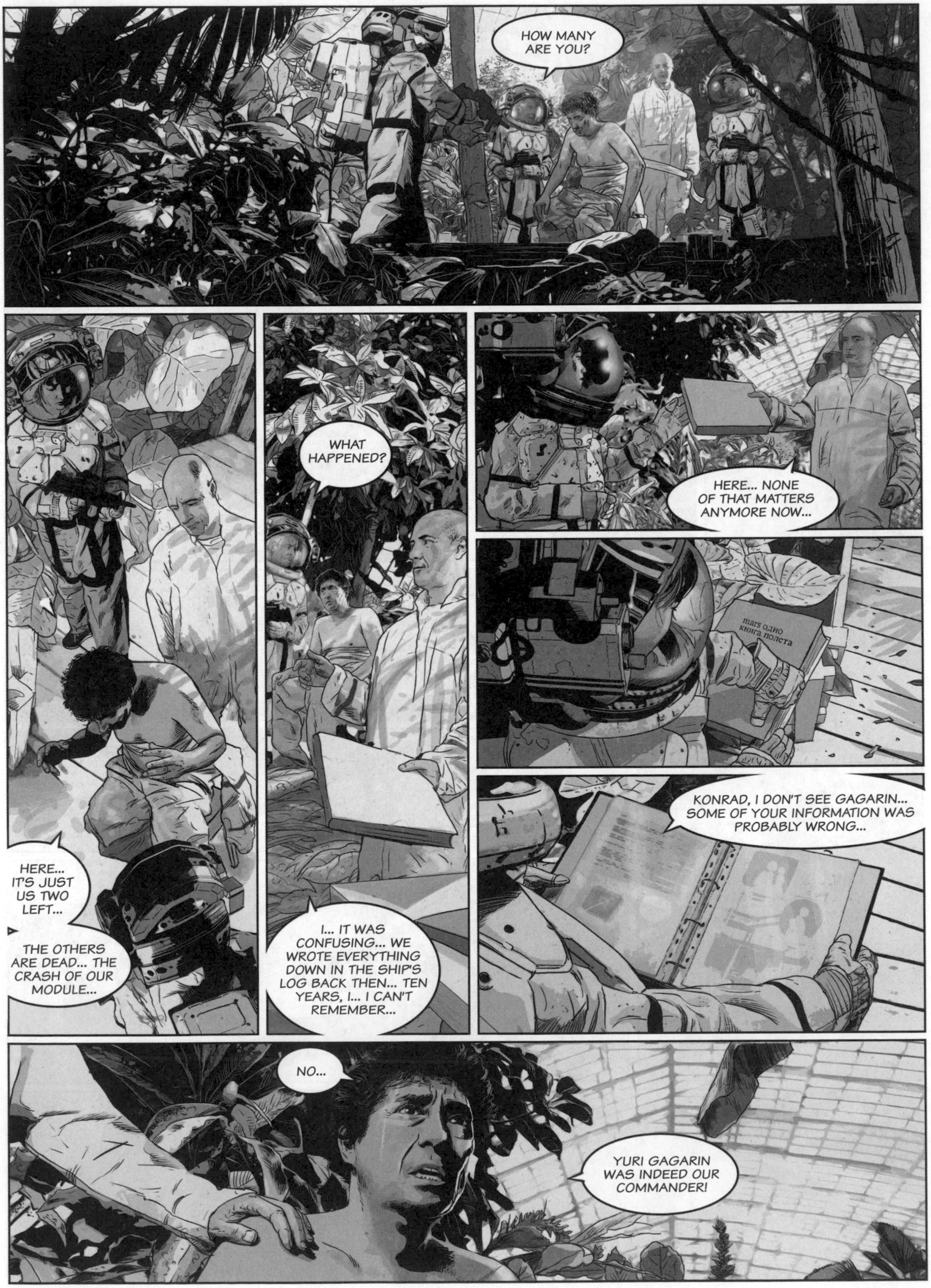
HOW MANY ARE YOU?
HERE... IT'S JUST US TWO LEFT...
THE OTHERS ARE DEAD... THE CRASH OF OUR MODULE...
WHAT HAPPENED?
I... IT WAS CONFUSING... WE WROTE EVERYTHING DOWN IN THE SHIP'S LOG BACK THEN... TEN YEARS, I... I CAN'T REMEMBER...
HERE... NONE OF THAT MATTERS ANYMORE NOW...
mars одно
книга полета
KONRAD, I DON'T SEE GAGARIN... SOME OF YOUR INFORMATION WAS PROBABLY WRONG...
NO...
YURI GAGARIN WAS INDEED OUR COMMANDER!

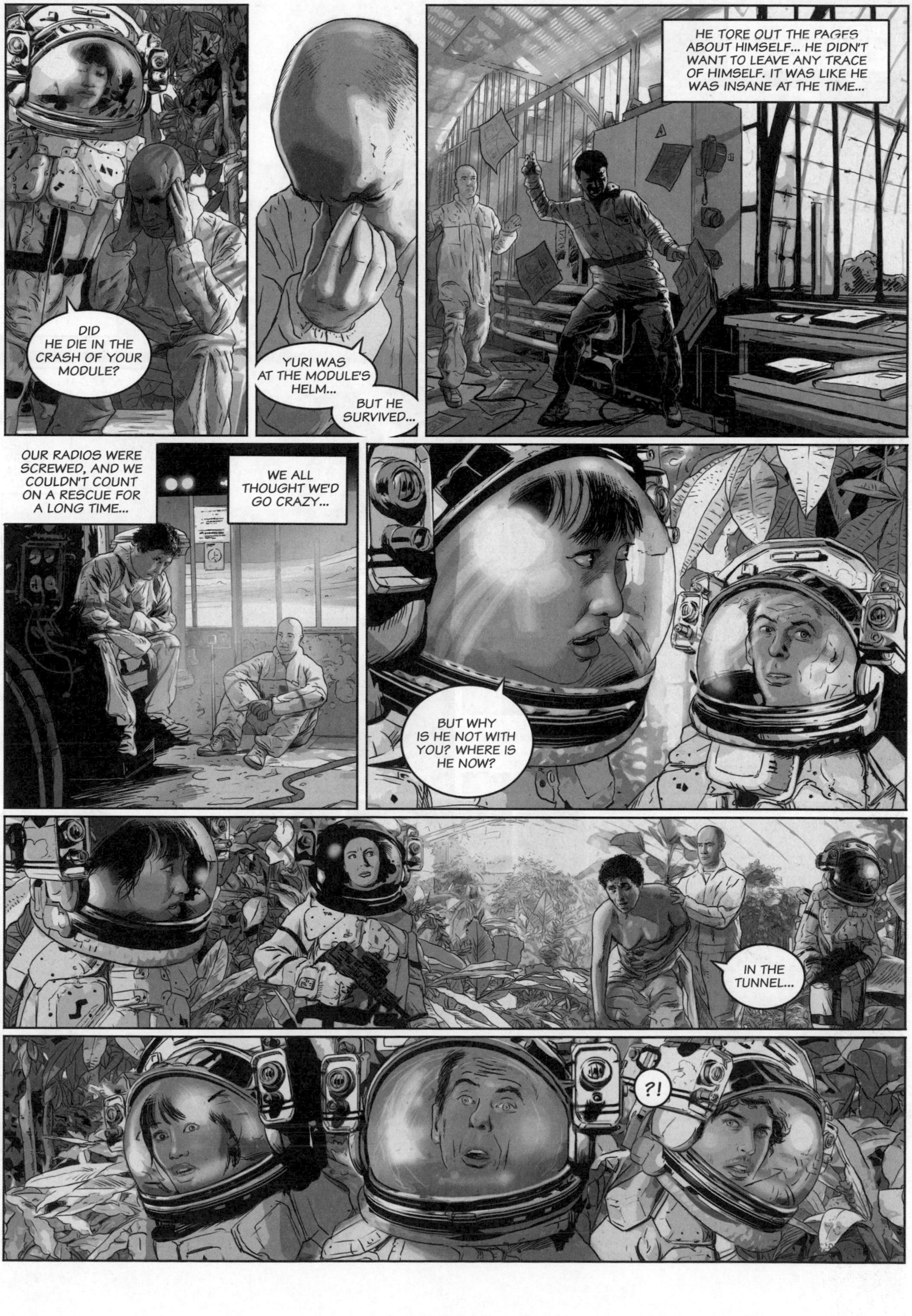
DID HE DIE IN THE CRASH OF YOUR MODULE?
YURI WAS AT THE MODULE'S HELM...
BUT HE SURVIVED...
HE TORE OUT THE PAGES ABOUT HIMSELF... HE DIDN'T WANT TO LEAVE ANY TRACE OF HIMSELF. IT WAS LIKE HE WAS INSANE AT THE TIME...
OUR RADIOS WERE SCREWED, AND WE COULDN'T COUNT ON A RESCUE FOR A LONG TIME...
WE ALL THOUGHT WE'D GO CRAZY...
BUT WHY IS HE NOT WITH YOU? WHERE IS HE NOW?
IN THE TUNNEL...
?!

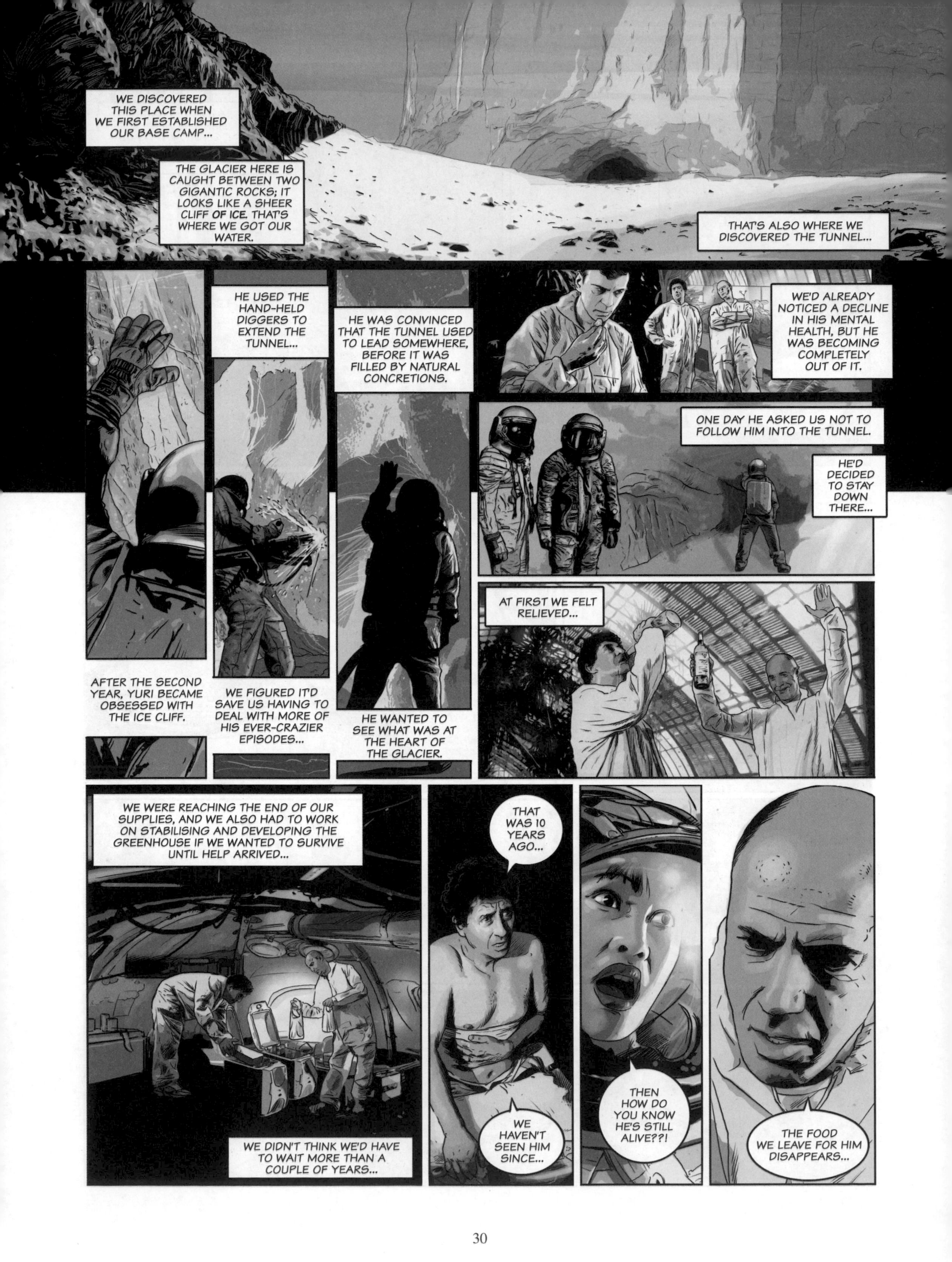

WE DISCOVERED THIS PLACE WHEN WE FIRST ESTABLISHED OUR BASE CAMP...
THE GLACIER HERE IS CAUGHT BETWEEN TWO GIGANTIC ROCKS; IT LOOKS LIKE A SHEER CLIFF OF ICE. THAT'S WHERE WE GOT OUR WATER.
THAT'S ALSO WHERE WE DISCOVERED THE TUNNEL...
AFTER THE SECOND YEAR, YURI BECAME OBSESSED WITH THE ICE CLIFF.
HE USED THE HAND-HELD DIGGERS TO EXTEND THE TUNNEL...
HE WAS CONVINCED THAT THE TUNNEL USED TO LEAD SOMEWHERE, BEFORE IT WAS FILLED BY NATURAL CONCRETIONS.
HE WANTED TO SEE WHAT WAS AT THE HEART OF THE GLACIER.
WE'D ALREADY NOTICED A DECLINE IN HIS MENTAL HEALTH, BUT HE WAS BECOMING COMPLETELY OUT OF IT.
ONE DAY HE ASKED US NOT TO FOLLOW HIM INTO THE TUNNEL.
HE'D DECIDED TO STAY DOWN THERE...
AT FIRST WE FELT RELIEVED...
WE FIGURED IT'D SAVE US HAVING TO DEAL WITH MORE OF HIS EVER-CRAZIER EPISODES...
WE WERE REACHING THE END OF OUR SUPPLIES, AND WE ALSO HAD TO WORK ON STABILISING AND DEVELOPING THE GREENHOUSE IF WE WANTED TO SURVIVE UNTIL HELP ARRIVED...
WE DIDN'T THINK WE'D HAVE TO WAIT MORE THAN A COUPLE OF YEARS...
THAT WAS 10 YEARS AGO...
WE HAVEN'T SEEN HIM SINCE...
THEN HOW DO YOU KNOW HE'S STILL ALIVE??!
THE FOOD WE LEAVE FOR HIM DISAPPEARS...

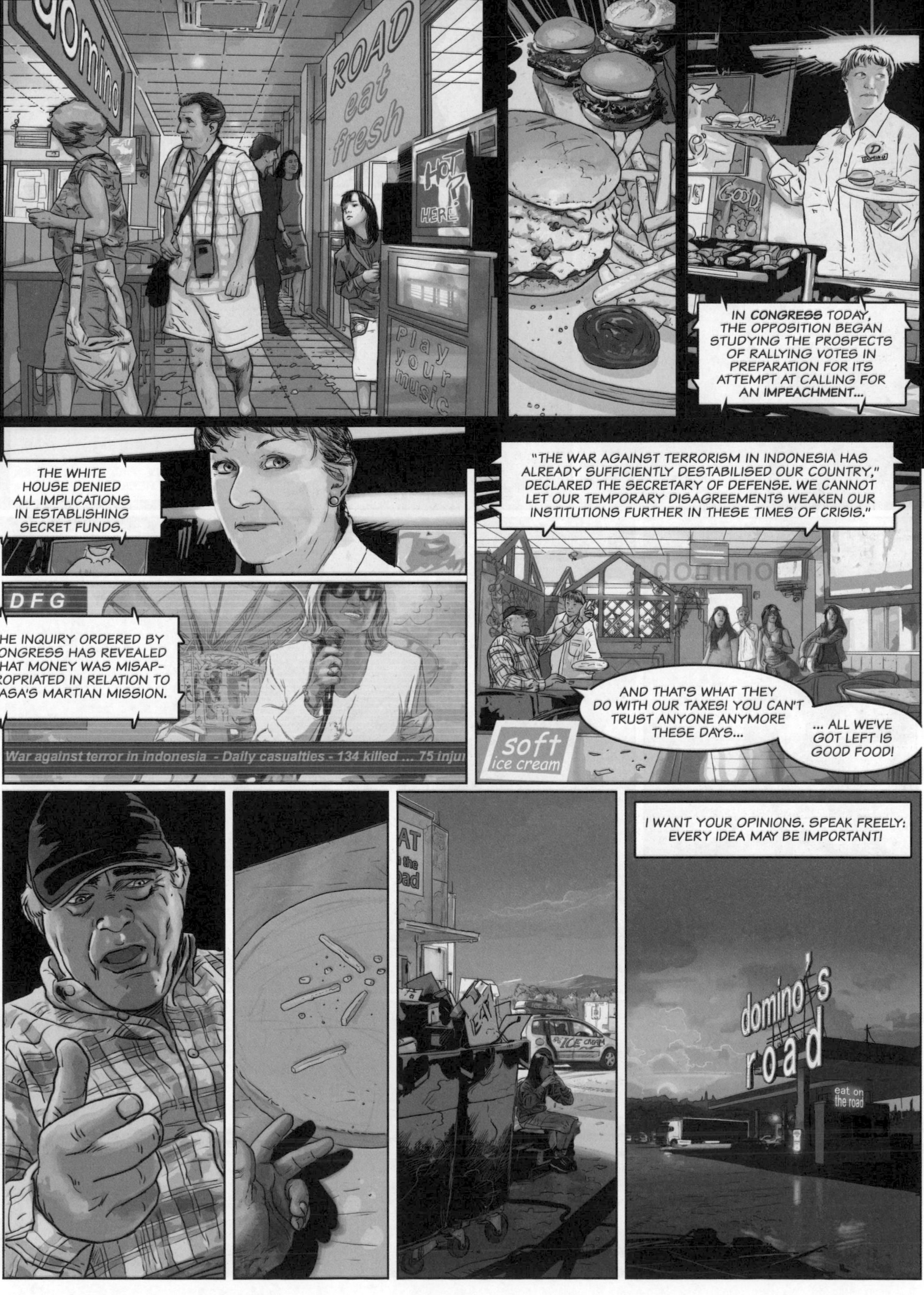
domino
ROAD eat fresh
HOT !? HERE!
Play your music
IN CONGRESS TODAY, THE OPPOSITION BEGAN STUDYING THE PROSPECTS OF RALLYING VOTES IN PREPARATION FOR ITS ATTEMPT AT CALLING FOR AN IMPEACHMENT...
THE WHITE HOUSE DENIED ALL IMPLICATIONS IN ESTABLISHING SECRET FUNDS.
DFG
THE INQUIRY ORDERED BY CONGRESS HAS REVEALED THAT MONEY WAS MISAP-PROPRIATED IN RELATION TO NASA'S MARTIAN MISSION.
War against terror in indonesia - Daily casualties - 134 killed ... 75 inju
"THE WAR AGAINST TERRORISM IN INDONESIA HAS ALREADY SUFFICIENTLY DESTABILISED OUR COUNTRY," DECLARED THE SECRETARY OF DEFENSE. WE CANNOT LET OUR TEMPORARY DISAGREEMENTS WEAKEN OUR INSTITUTIONS FURTHER IN THESE TIMES OF CRISIS."
domino
AND THAT'S WHAT THEY DO WITH OUR TAXES! YOU CAN'T TRUST ANYONE ANYMORE THESE DAYS...
... ALL WE'VE GOT LEFT IS GOOD FOOD!
soft ice cream
I WANT YOUR OPINIONS. SPEAK FREELY: EVERY IDEA MAY BE IMPORTANT!
domino's road
eat on the road

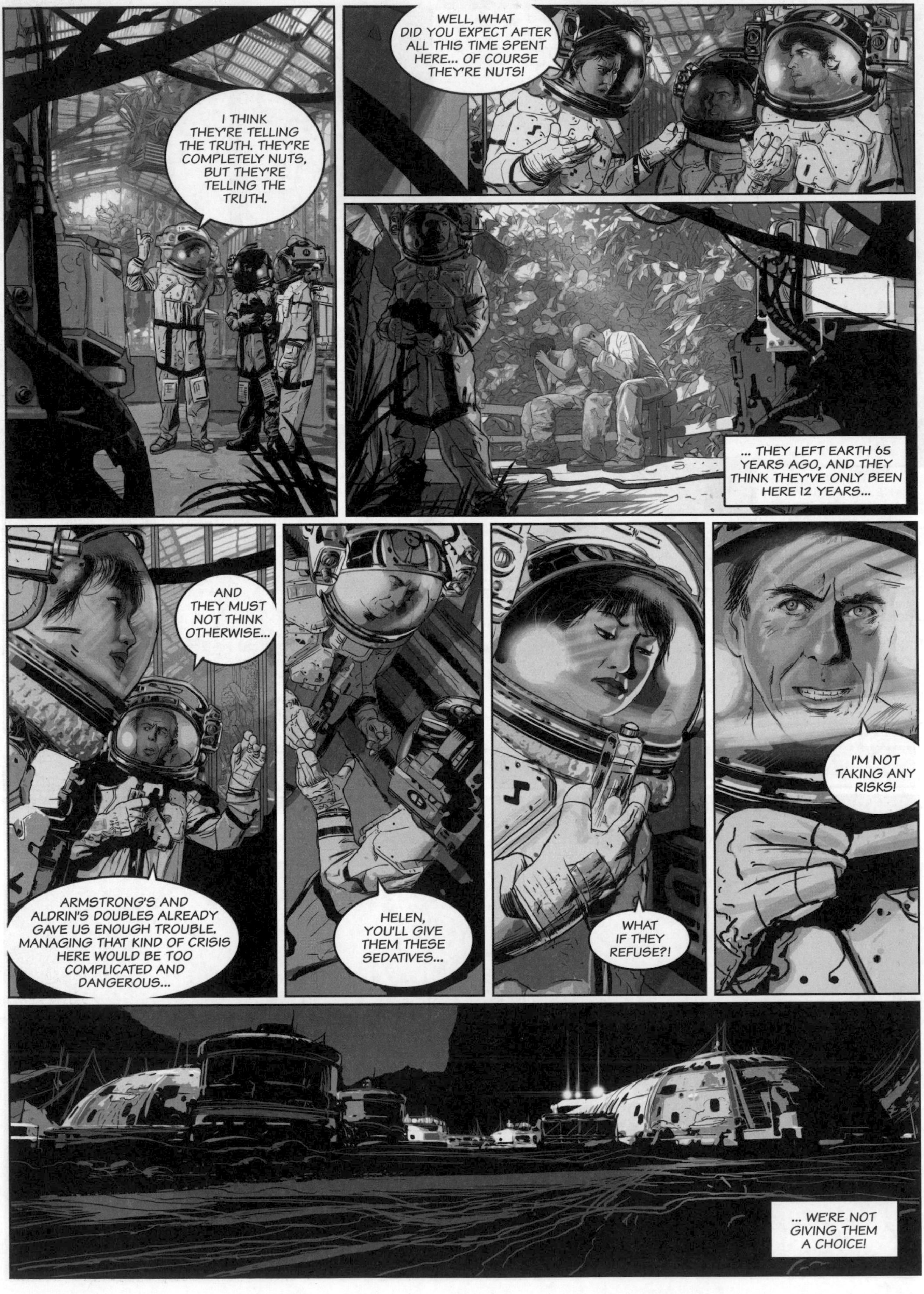
I THINK THEY'RE TELLING THE TRUTH. THEY'RE COMPLETELY NUTS, BUT THEY'RE TELLING THE TRUTH.
WELL, WHAT DID YOU EXPECT AFTER ALL THIS TIME SPENT HERE... OF COURSE THEY'RE NUTS!
... THEY LEFT EARTH 65 YEARS AGO, AND THEY THINK THEY'VE ONLY BEEN HERE 12 YEARS...
AND THEY MUST NOT THINK OTHERWISE...
ARMSTRONG'S AND ALDRIN'S DOUBLES ALREADY GAVE US ENOUGH TROUBLE. MANAGING THAT KIND OF CRISIS HERE WOULD BE TOO COMPLICATED AND DANGEROUS...
HELEN, YOU'LL GIVE THEM THESE SEDATIVES...
WHAT IF THEY REFUSE?!
I'M NOT TAKING ANY RISKS!
... WE'RE NOT GIVING THEM A CHOICE!

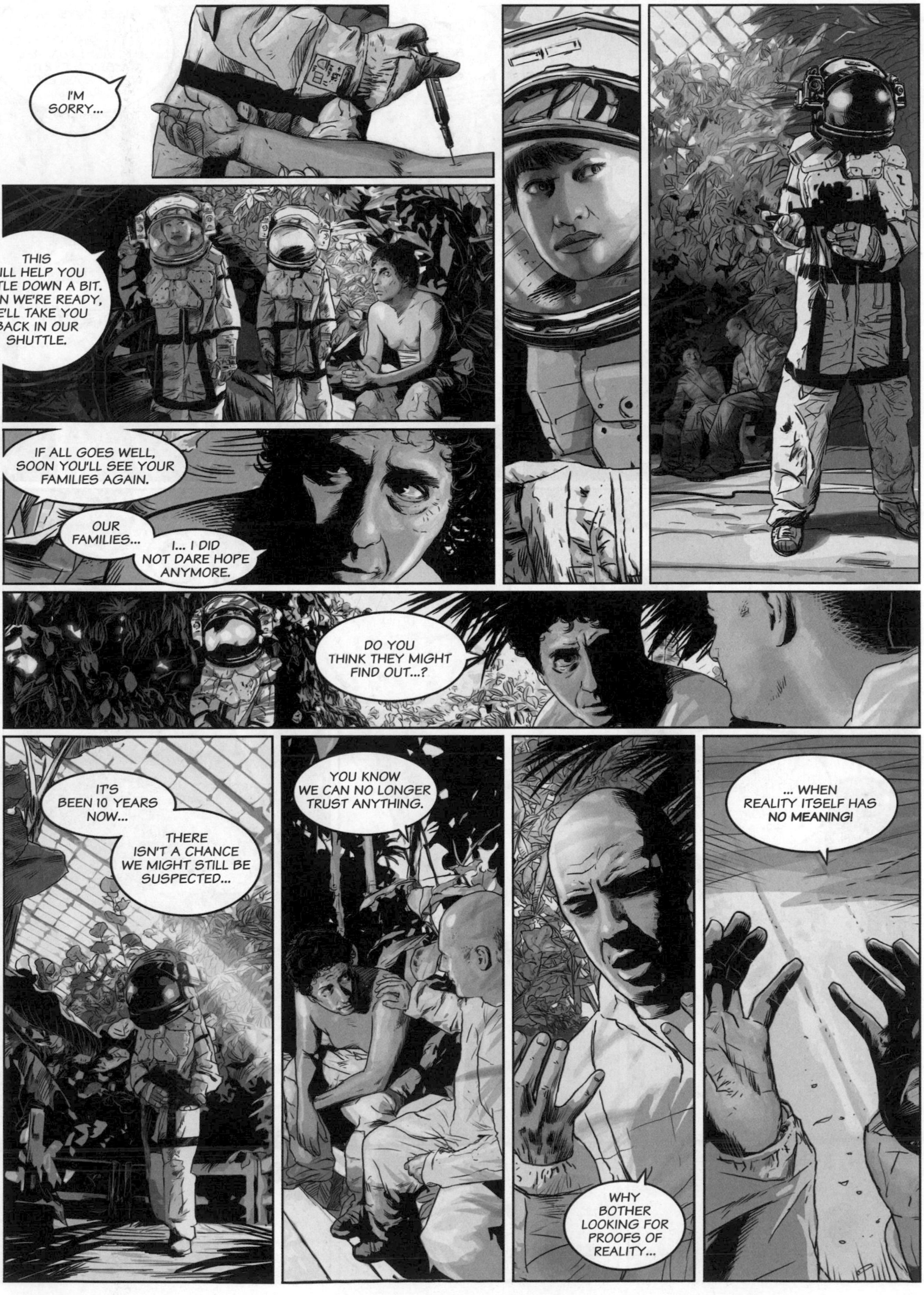
I'M SORRY...
THIS WILL HELP YOU SETTLE DOWN A BIT. WHEN WE'RE READY, WE'LL TAKE YOU BACK IN OUR SHUTTLE.
IF ALL GOES WELL, SOON YOU'LL SEE YOUR FAMILIES AGAIN.
OUR FAMILIES...
I... I DID NOT DARE HOPE ANYMORE.
DO YOU THINK THEY MIGHT FIND OUT...?
IT'S BEEN 10 YEARS NOW...
THERE ISN'T A CHANCE WE MIGHT STILL BE SUSPECTED...
YOU KNOW WE CAN NO LONGER TRUST ANYTHING.
WHY BOTHER LOOKING FOR PROOFS OF REALITY...
... WHEN REALITY ITSELF HAS NO MEANING!

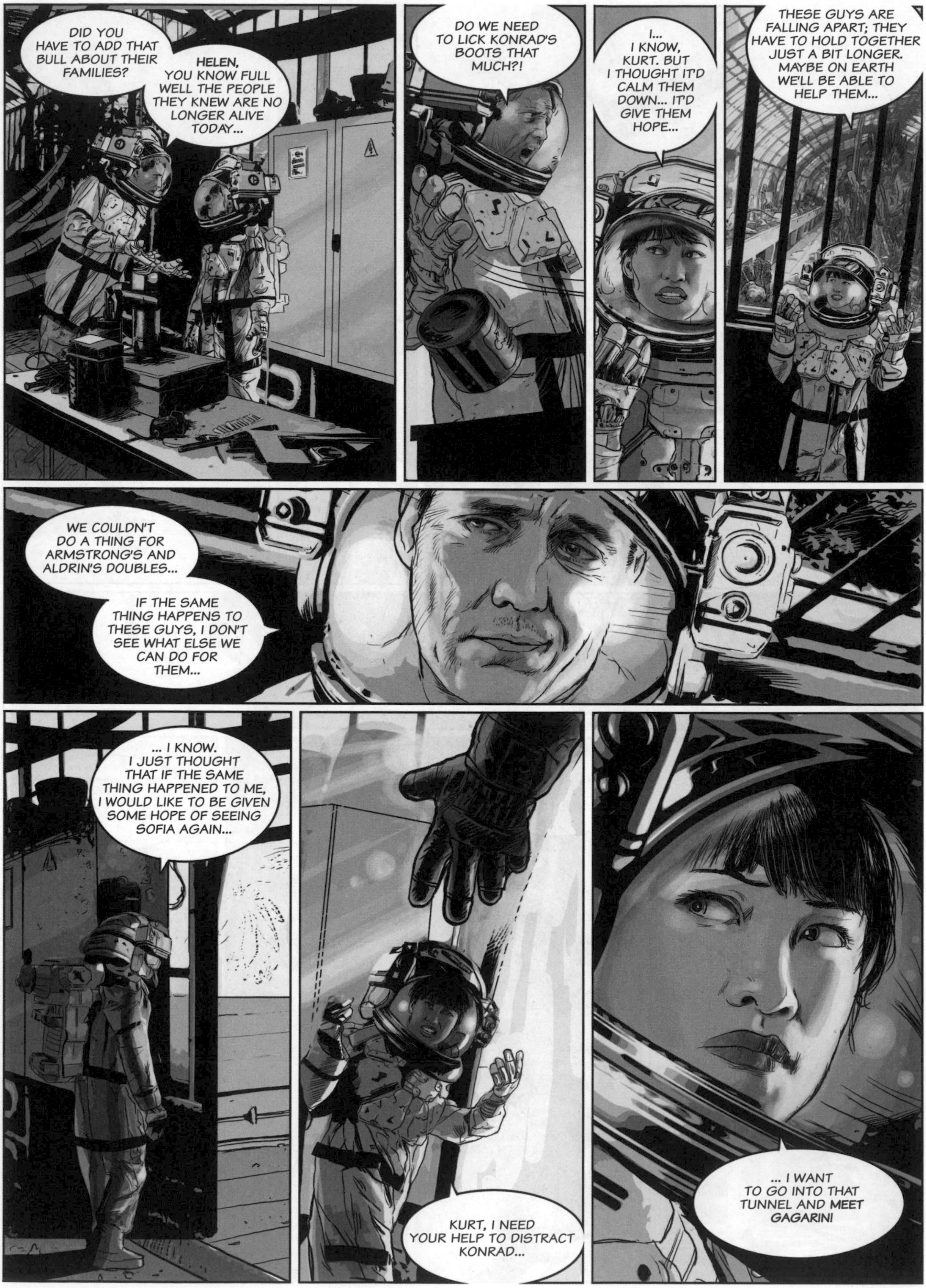
DID YOU HAVE TO ADD THAT BULL ABOUT THEIR FAMILIES?
HELEN, YOU KNOW FULL WELL THE PEOPLE THEY KNEW ARE NO LONGER ALIVE TODAY...
DO WE NEED TO LICK KONRAD'S BOOTS THAT MUCH?!
I... I KNOW, KURT. BUT I THOUGHT IT'D CALM THEM DOWN... IT'D GIVE THEM HOPE...
THESE GUYS ARE FALLING APART; THEY HAVE TO HOLD TOGETHER JUST A BIT LONGER. MAYBE ON EARTH WE'LL BE ABLE TO HELP THEM...
WE COULDN'T DO A THING FOR ARMSTRONG'S AND ALDRIN'S DOUBLES...
IF THE SAME THING HAPPENS TO THESE GUYS, I DON'T SEE WHAT ELSE WE CAN DO FOR THEM...
... I KNOW. I JUST THOUGHT THAT IF THE SAME THING HAPPENED TO ME, I WOULD LIKE TO BE GIVEN SOME HOPE OF SEEING SOFIA AGAIN...
KURT, I NEED YOUR HELP TO DISTRACT KONRAD...
... I WANT TO GO INTO THAT TUNNEL AND MEET GAGARIN!

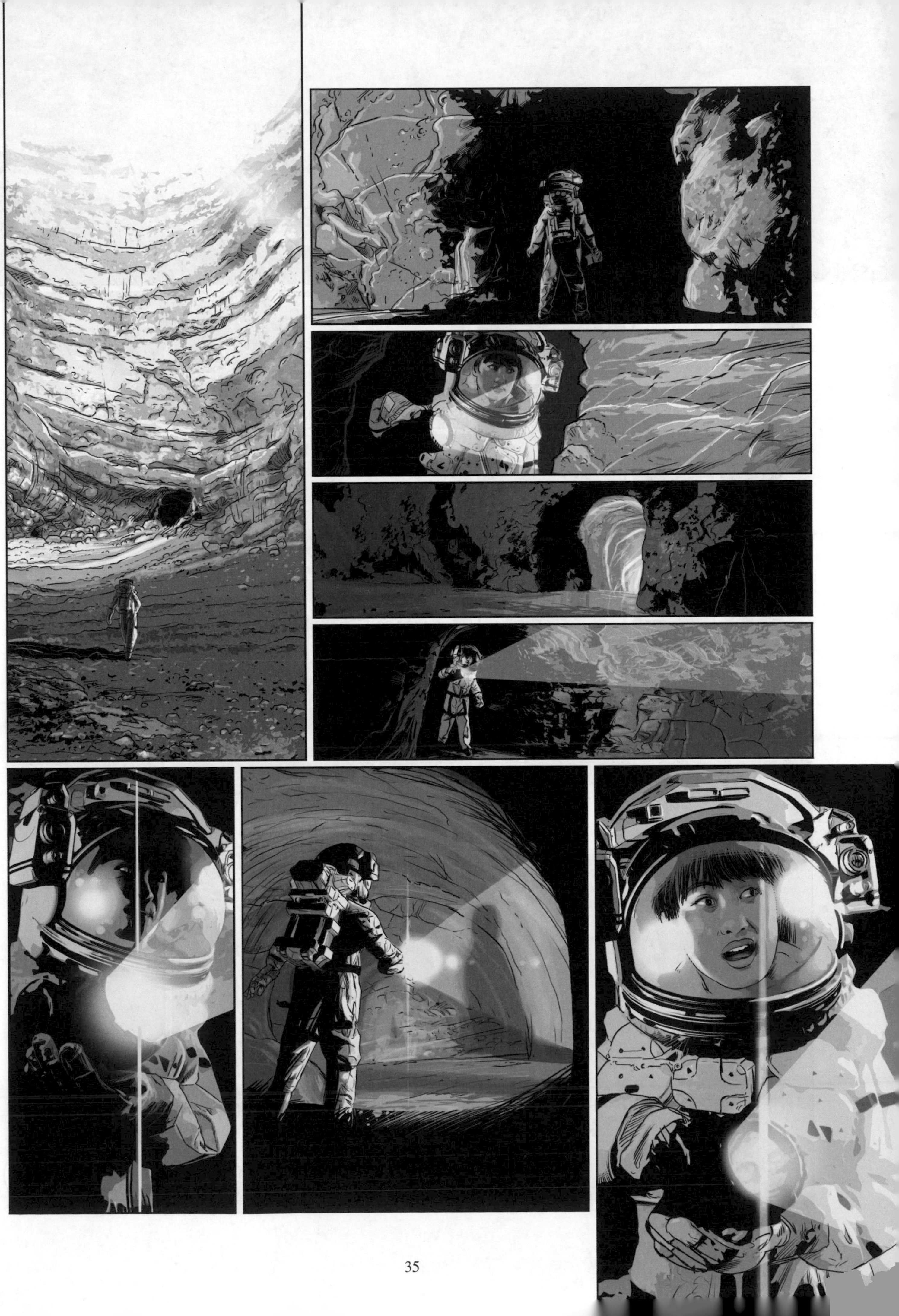

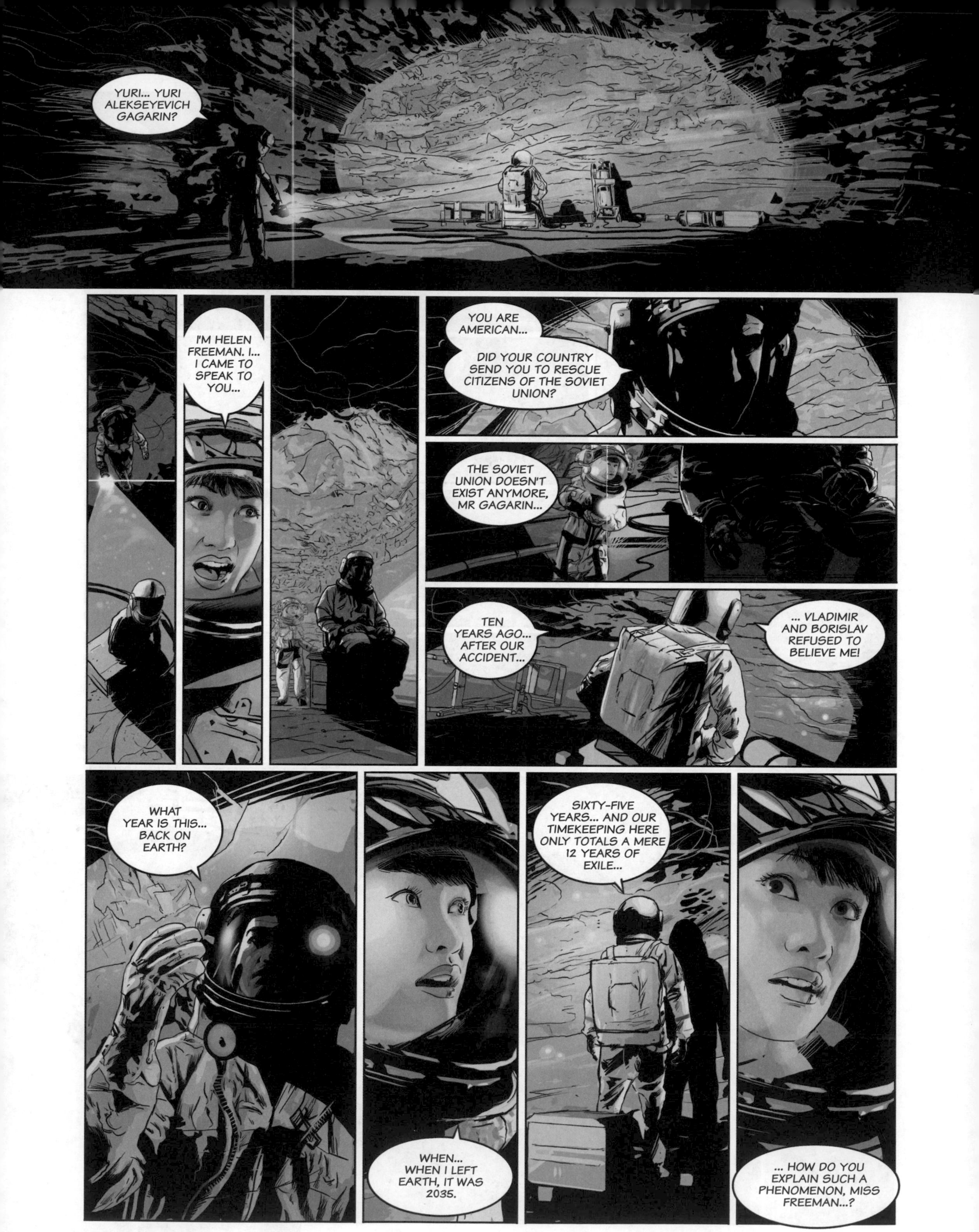
YURI... YURI ALEKSEYEVICH GAGARIN?
I'M HELEN FREEMAN. I... I CAME TO SPEAK TO YOU...
YOU ARE AMERICAN...
DID YOUR COUNTRY SEND YOU TO RESCUE CITIZENS OF THE SOVIET UNION?
THE SOVIET UNION DOESN'T EXIST ANYMORE, MR GAGARIN...
TEN YEARS AGO... AFTER OUR ACCIDENT...
... VLADIMIR AND BORISLAV REFUSED TO BELIEVE ME!
WHAT YEAR IS THIS... BACK ON EARTH?
WHEN... WHEN I LEFT EARTH, IT WAS 2035.
SIXTY-FIVE YEARS... AND OUR TIMEKEEPING HERE ONLY TOTALS A MERE 12 YEARS OF EXILE...
... HOW DO YOU EXPLAIN SUCH A PHENOMENON, MISS FREEMAN...?

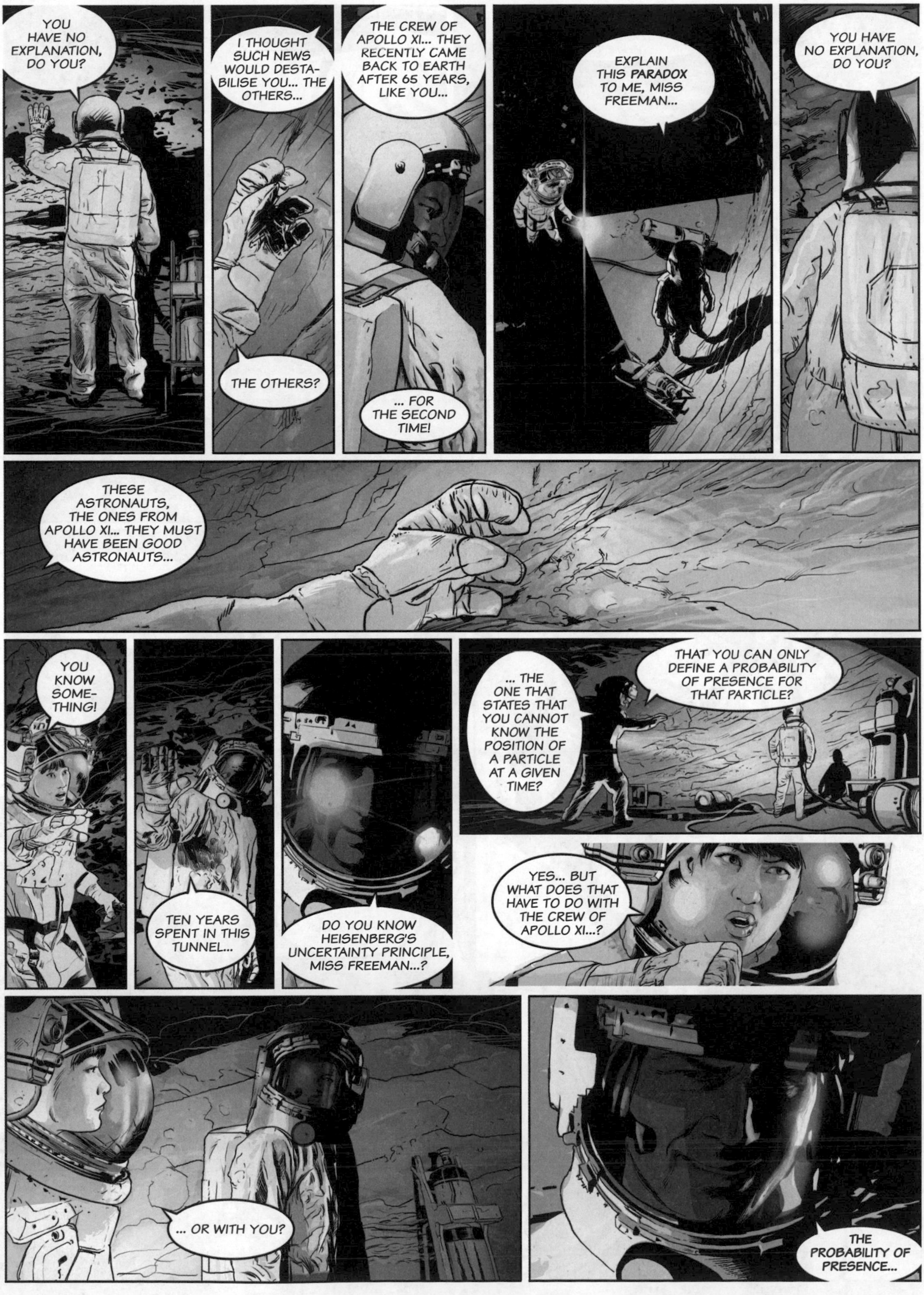
YOU HAVE NO EXPLANATION, DO YOU?
I THOUGHT SUCH NEWS WOULD DESTA-BILISE YOU... THE OTHERS...
THE OTHERS?
THE CREW OF APOLLO XI... THEY RECENTLY CAME BACK TO EARTH AFTER 65 YEARS, LIKE YOU...
... FOR THE SECOND TIME!
EXPLAIN THIS PARADOX TO ME, MISS FREEMAN...
YOU HAVE NO EXPLANATION, DO YOU?
THESE ASTRONAUTS, THE ONES FROM APOLLO XI... THEY MUST HAVE BEEN GOOD ASTRONAUTS...
YOU KNOW SOME-THING!
TEN YEARS SPENT IN THIS TUNNEL...
DO YOU KNOW HEISENBERG'S UNCERTAINTY PRINCIPLE, MISS FREEMAN...?
... THE ONE THAT STATES THAT YOU CANNOT KNOW THE POSITION OF A PARTICLE AT A GIVEN TIME?
THAT YOU CAN ONLY DEFINE A PROBABILITY OF PRESENCE FOR THAT PARTICLE?
YES... BUT WHAT DOES THAT HAVE TO DO WITH THE CREW OF APOLLO XI...?
... OR WITH YOU?
THE PROBABILITY OF PRESENCE...

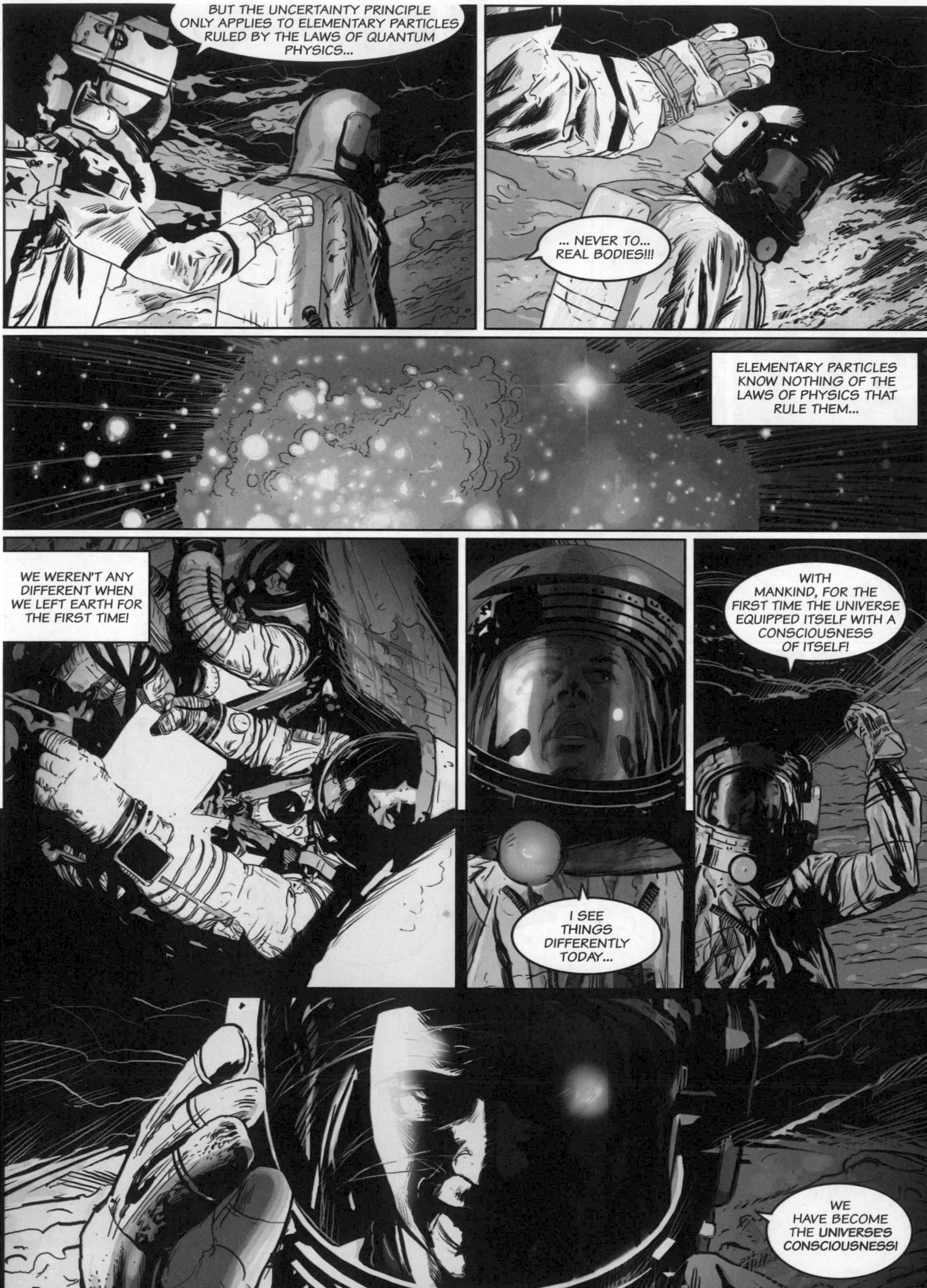
BUT THE UNCERTAINTY PRINCIPLE ONLY APPLIES TO ELEMENTARY PARTICLES RULED BY THE LAWS OF QUANTUM PHYSICS...
... NEVER TO... REAL BODIES!!!
ELEMENTARY PARTICLES KNOW NOTHING OF THE LAWS OF PHYSICS THAT RULE THEM...
WE WEREN'T ANY DIFFERENT WHEN WE LEFT EARTH FOR THE FIRST TIME!
I SEE THINGS DIFFERENTLY TODAY...
WITH MANKIND, FOR THE FIRST TIME THE UNIVERSE EQUIPPED ITSELF WITH A CONSCIOUSNESS OF ITSELF!
WE HAVE BECOME THE UNIVERSE'S CONSCIOUSNESS!

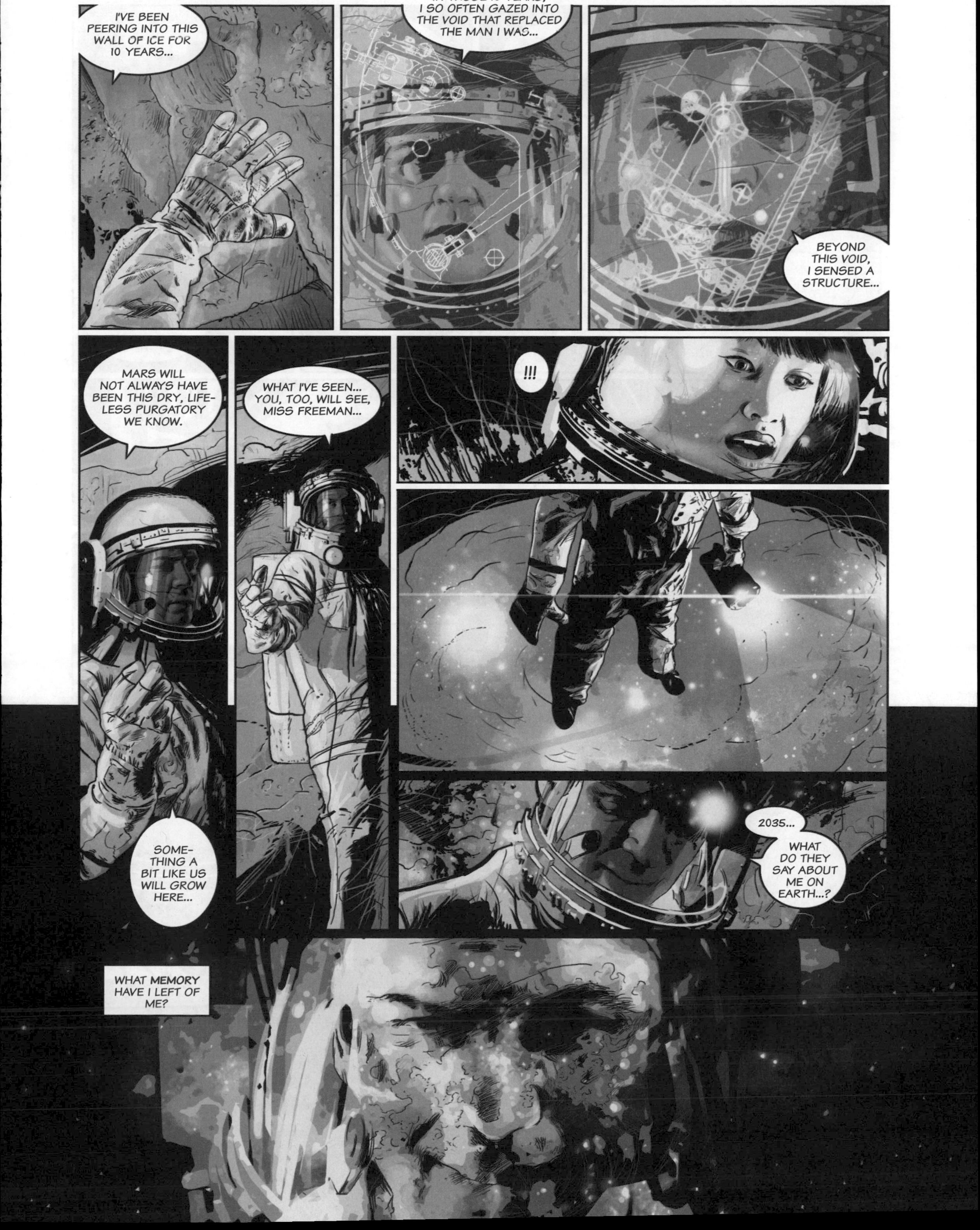
I'VE BEEN PEERING INTO THIS WALL OF ICE FOR 10 YEARS...
IN THOSE 10 YEARS, I SO OFTEN GAZED INTO THE VOID THAT REPLACED THE MAN I WAS...
BEYOND THIS VOID, I SENSED A STRUCTURE...
MARS WILL NOT ALWAYS HAVE BEEN THIS DRY, LIFE-LESS PURGATORY WE KNOW.
SOME-THING A BIT LIKE US WILL GROW HERE...
WHAT I'VE SEEN... YOU, TOO, WILL SEE, MISS FREEMAN...
!!!
2035...
WHAT DO THEY SAY ABOUT ME ON EARTH...?
WHAT MEMORY HAVE I LEFT OF ME?

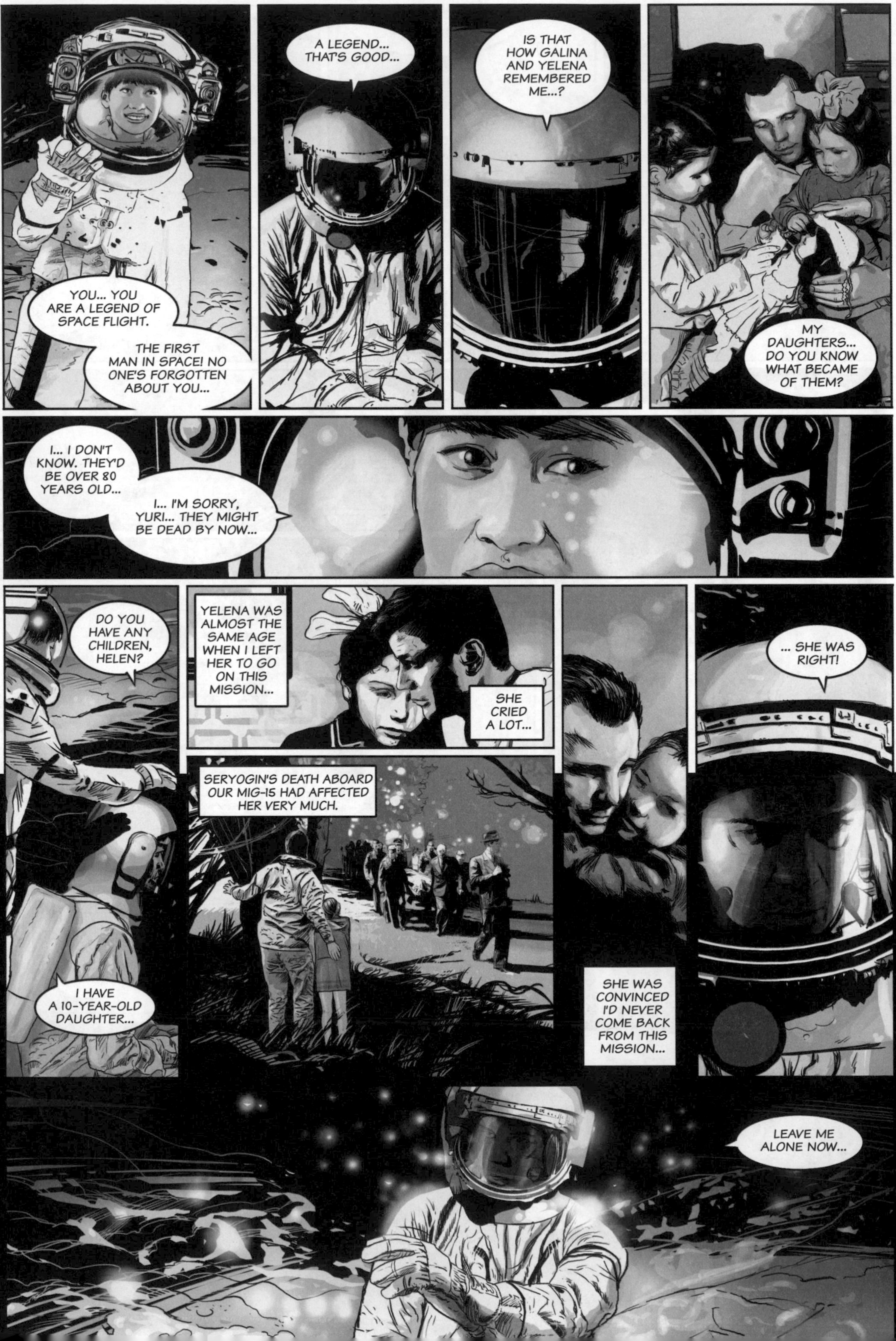
A LEGEND... THAT'S GOOD...
IS THAT HOW GALINA AND YELENA REMEMBERED ME...?
YOU... YOU ARE A LEGEND OF SPACE FLIGHT.
THE FIRST MAN IN SPACE! NO ONE'S FORGOTTEN ABOUT YOU...
MY DAUGHTERS... DO YOU KNOW WHAT BECAME OF THEM?
I... I DON'T KNOW. THEY'D BE OVER 80 YEARS OLD...
I... I'M SORRY, YURI... THEY MIGHT BE DEAD BY NOW...
DO YOU HAVE ANY CHILDREN, HELEN?
I HAVE A 10-YEAR-OLD DAUGHTER...
YELENA WAS ALMOST THE SAME AGE WHEN I LEFT HER TO GO ON THIS MISSION...
SHE CRIED A LOT...
SERYOGIN'S DEATH ABOARD OUR MIG-15 HAD AFFECTED HER VERY MUCH.
SHE WAS CONVINCED I'D NEVER COME BACK FROM THIS MISSION...
... SHE WAS RIGHT!
LEAVE ME ALONE NOW...

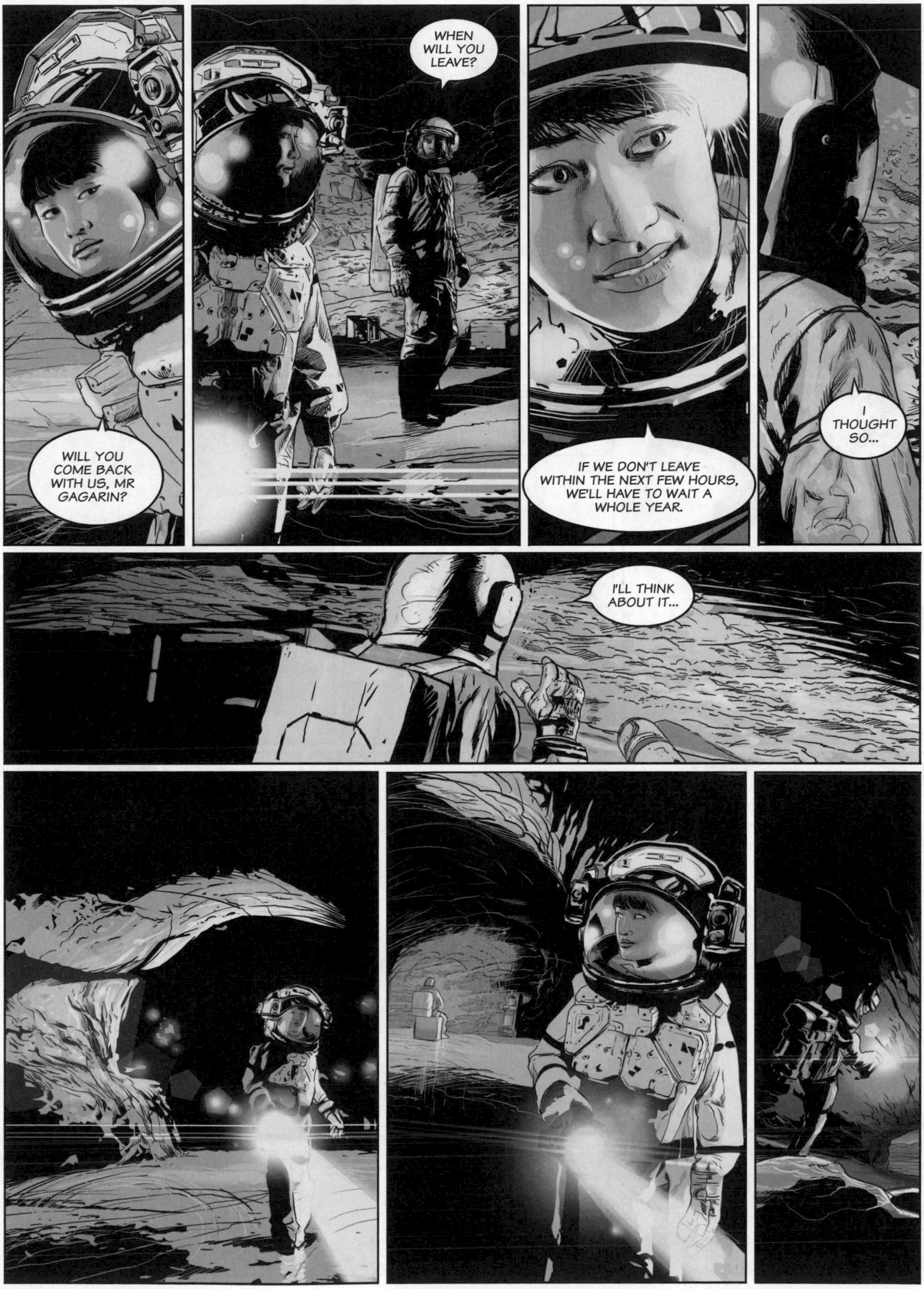
WILL YOU COME BACK WITH US, MR GAGARIN?
WHEN WILL YOU LEAVE?
IF WE DON'T LEAVE WITHIN THE NEXT FEW HOURS, WE'LL HAVE TO WAIT A WHOLE YEAR.
I THOUGHT SO...
I'LL THINK ABOUT IT...

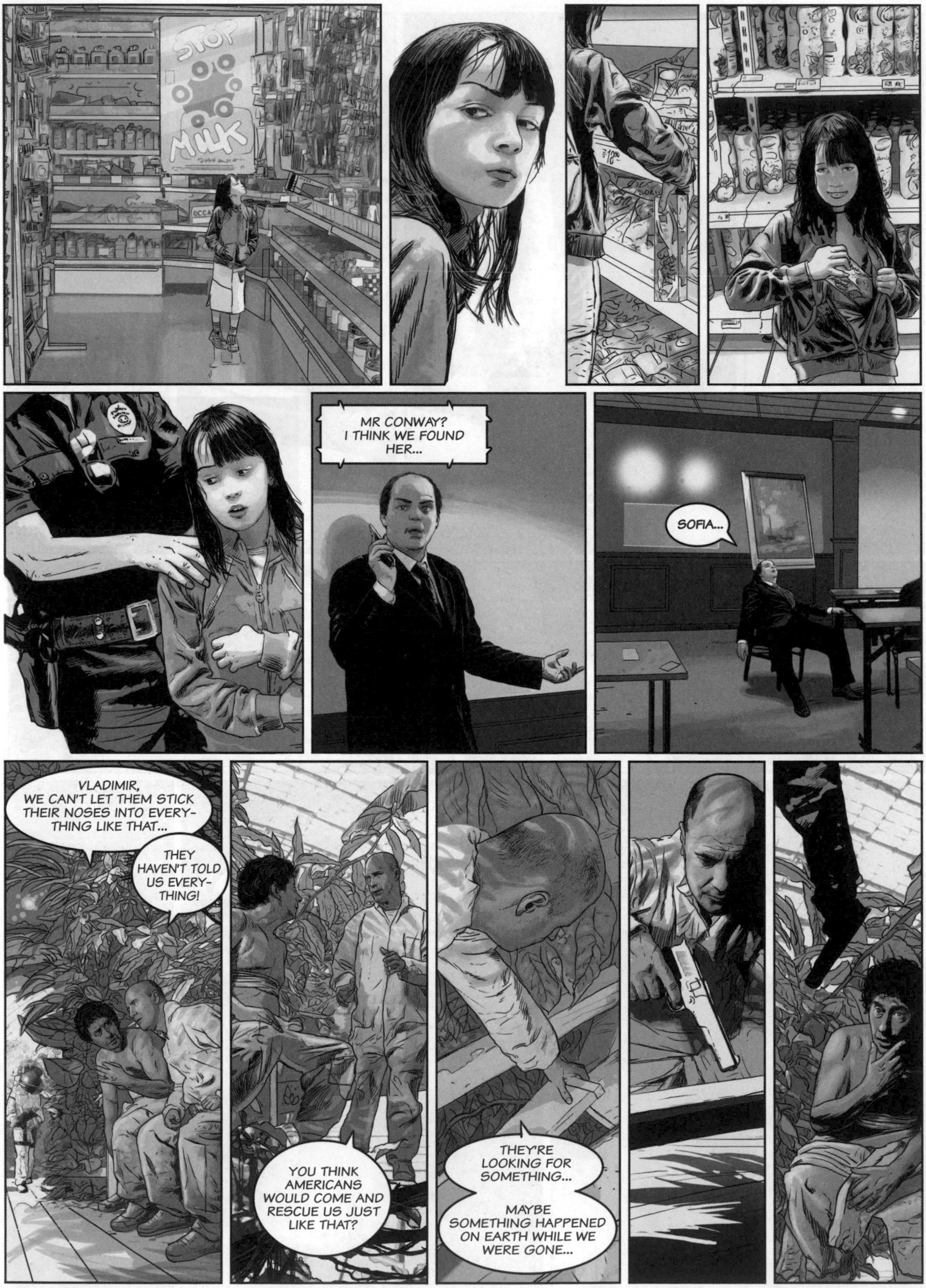
STOP MILK
MR CONWAY? I THINK WE FOUND HER...
SOFIA...
VLADIMIR, WE CAN'T LET THEM STICK THEIR NOSES INTO EVERY-THING LIKE THAT...
THEY HAVEN'T TOLD US EVERY-THING!
YOU THINK AMERICANS WOULD COME AND RESCUE US JUST LIKE THAT?
THEY'RE LOOKING FOR SOMETHING...
MAYBE SOMETHING HAPPENED ON EARTH WHILE WE WERE GONE...

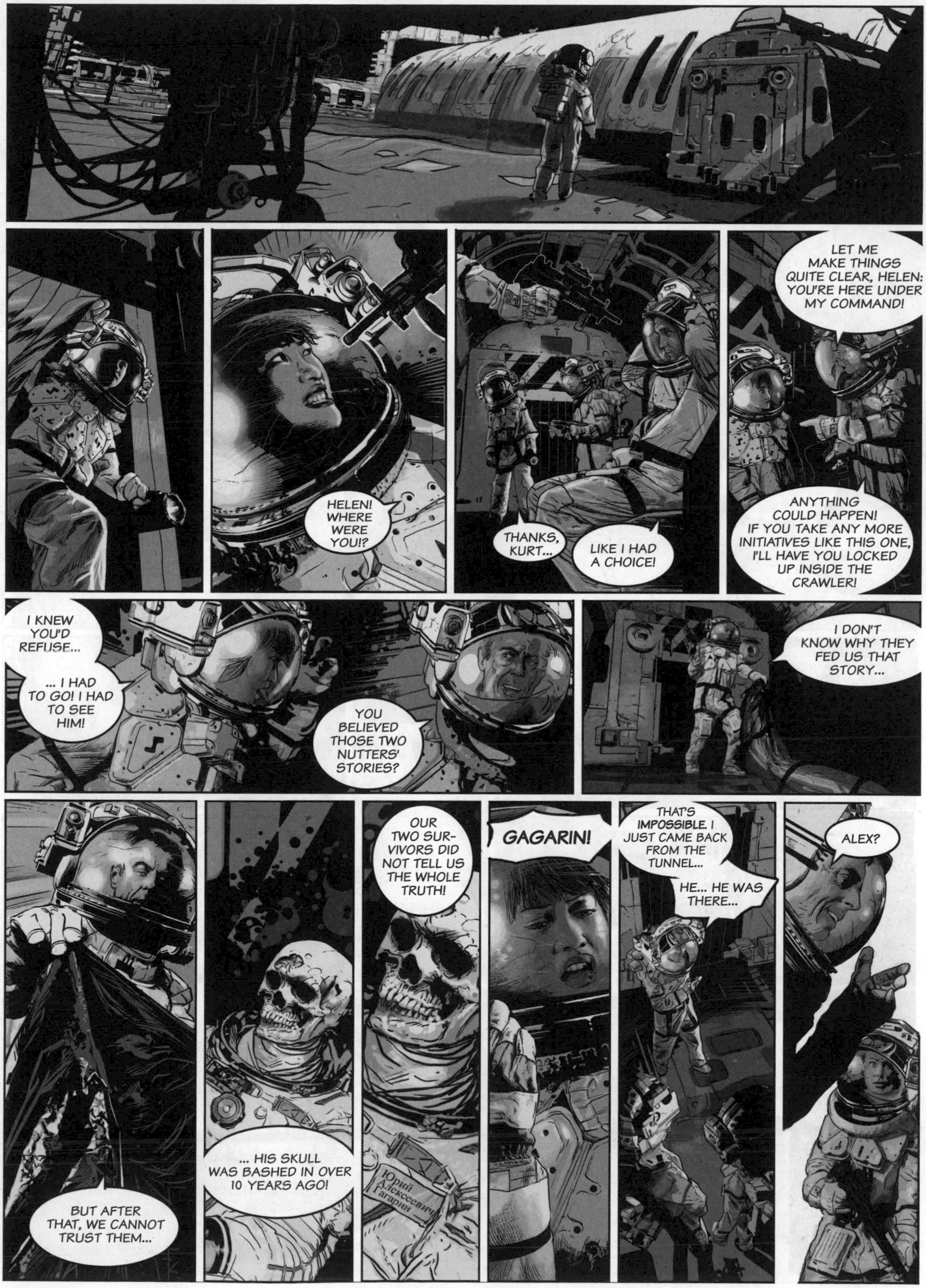
HELEN! WHERE WERE YOU!?
THANKS, KURT...
LIKE I HAD A CHOICE!
LET ME MAKE THINGS QUITE CLEAR, HELEN: YOU'RE HERE UNDER MY COMMAND!
ANYTHING COULD HAPPEN! IF YOU TAKE ANY MORE INITIATIVES LIKE THIS ONE, I'LL HAVE YOU LOCKED UP INSIDE THE CRAWLER!
I KNEW YOU'D REFUSE...
... I HAD TO GO! I HAD TO SEE HIM!
YOU BELIEVED THOSE TWO NUTTERS' STORIES?
I DON'T KNOW WHY THEY FED US THAT STORY...
BUT AFTER THAT, WE CANNOT TRUST THEM...
... HIS SKULL WAS BASHED IN OVER 10 YEARS AGO!
OUR TWO SURVIVORS DID NOT TELL US THE WHOLE TRUTH!
Юрий Алексеевич Гагарин
GAGARIN!
THAT'S IMPOSSIBLE. I JUST CAME BACK FROM THE TUNNEL...
HE... HE WAS THERE...
ALEX?

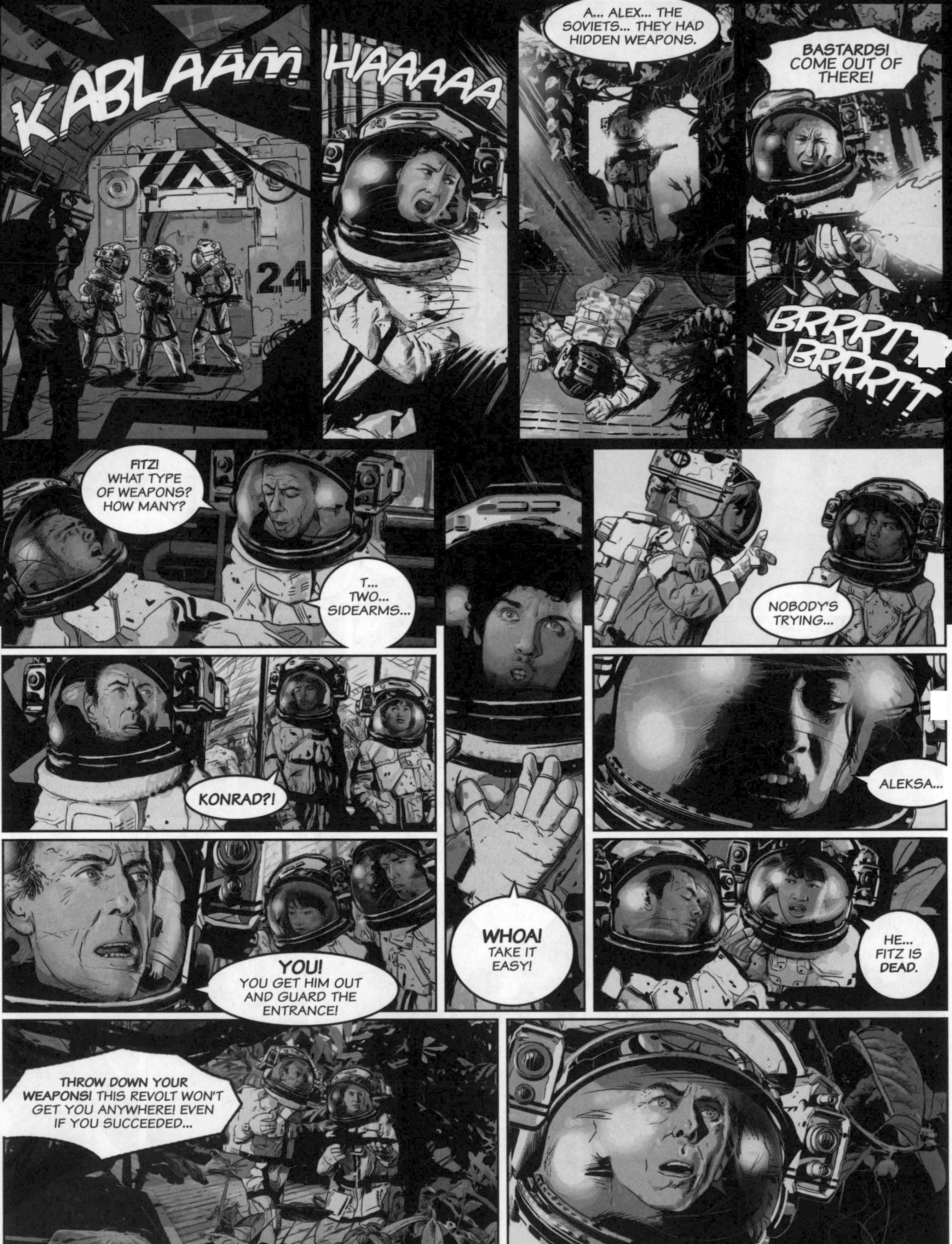
KABLAAM
HAAAAA
A... ALEX... THE SOVIETS... THEY HAD HIDDEN WEAPONS.
BASTARDS! COME OUT OF THERE!
BRRRT!! BRRRT!!
FITZ! WHAT TYPE OF WEAPONS? HOW MANY?
T... TWO... SIDEARMS...
NOBODY'S TRYING...
KONRAD?!
ALEKSA...
YOU! YOU GET HIM OUT AND GUARD THE ENTRANCE!
WHOA! TAKE IT EASY!
HE... FITZ IS DEAD.
THROW DOWN YOUR WEAPONS! THIS REVOLT WON'T GET YOU ANYWHERE! EVEN IF YOU SUCCEEDED...

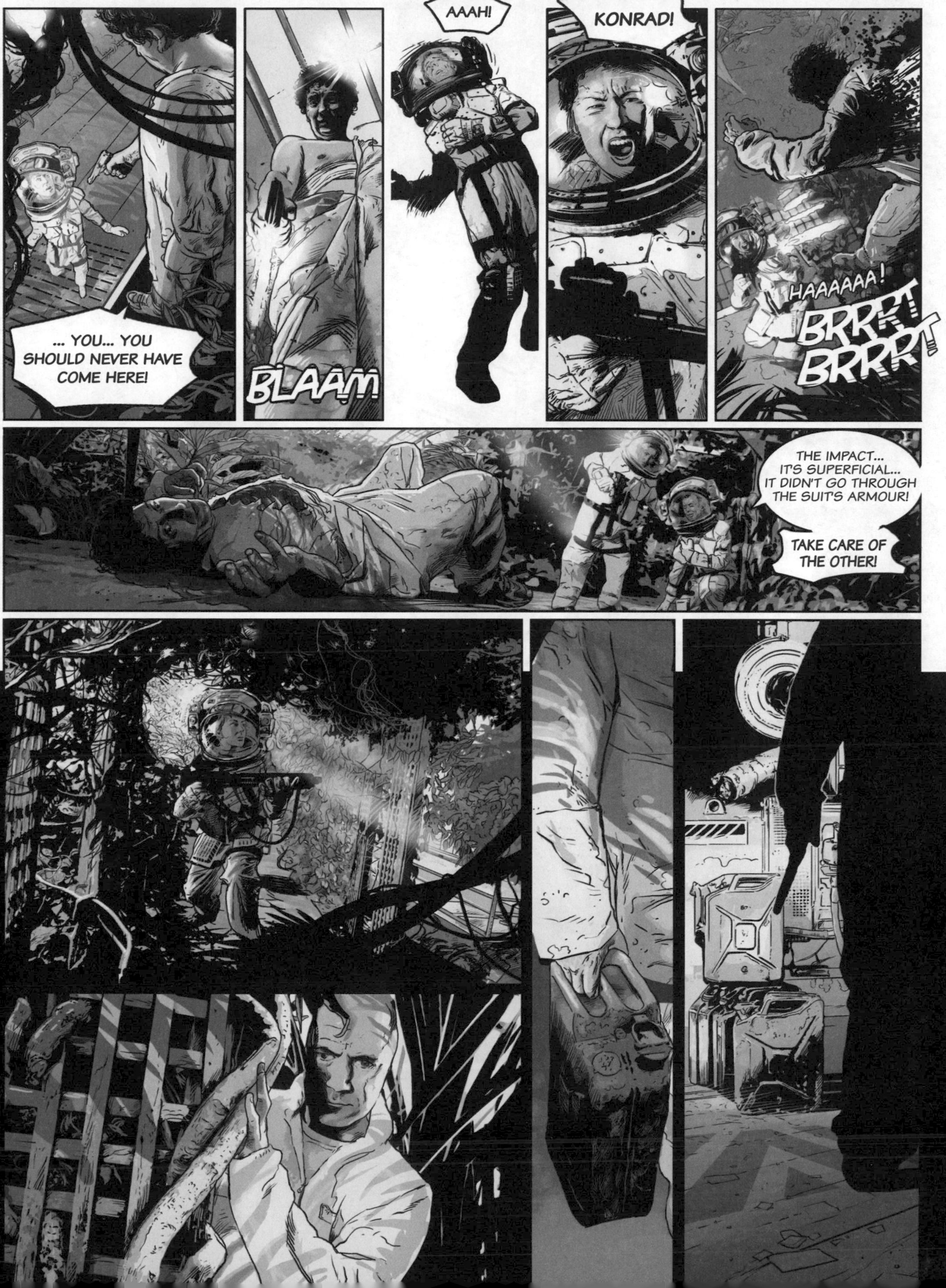
... YOU... YOU SHOULD NEVER HAVE COME HERE!
BLAAM
AAAH!
KONRAD!
HAAAAAA!
BRRRT BRRRT!
THE IMPACT... IT'S SUPERFICIAL... IT DIDN'T GO THROUGH THE SUIT'S ARMOUR!
TAKE CARE OF THE OTHER!

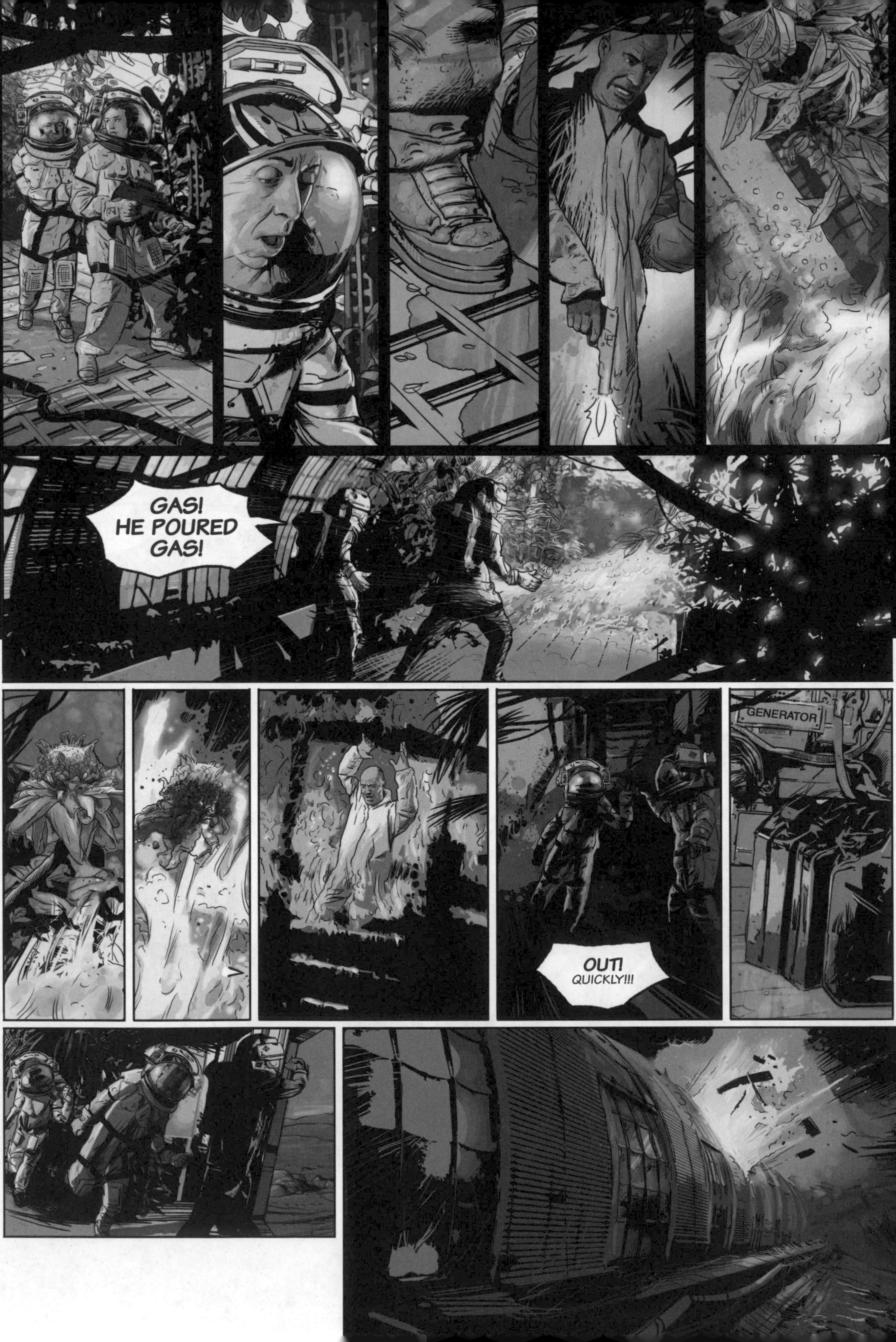
GAS! HE POURED GAS!
GENERATOR
OUT! QUICKLY!!!

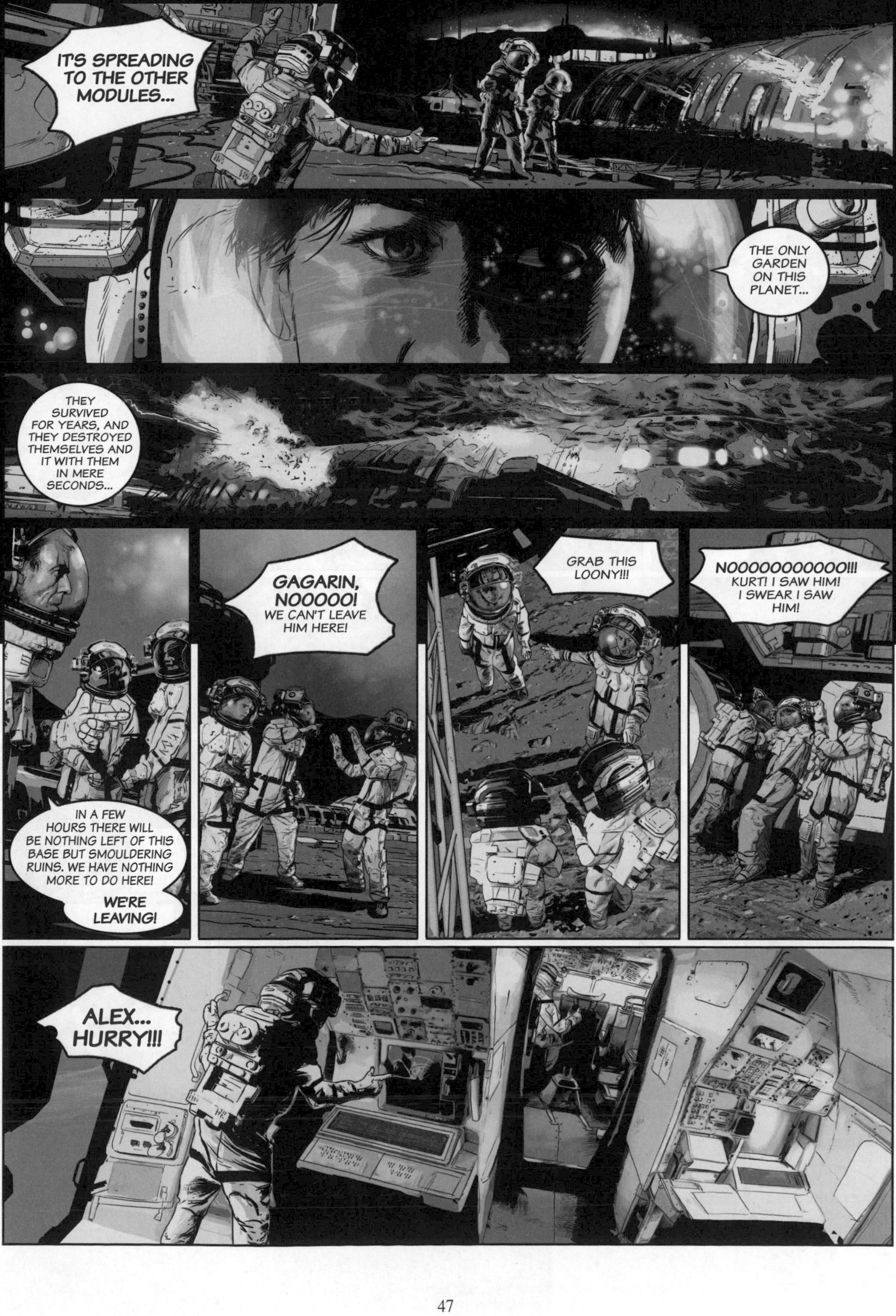
IT'S SPREADING TO THE OTHER MODULES...
THE ONLY GARDEN ON THIS PLANET...
THEY SURVIVED FOR YEARS, AND THEY DESTROYED THEMSELVES AND IT WITH THEM IN MERE SECONDS...
IN A FEW HOURS THERE WILL BE NOTHING LEFT OF THIS BASE BUT SMOULDERING RUINS. WE HAVE NOTHING MORE TO DO HERE!
WE'RE LEAVING!
GAGARIN, NOOOOO! WE CAN'T LEAVE HIM HERE!
GRAB THIS LOONY!!!
NOOOOOOOOOOO!!! KURT! I SAW HIM! I SWEAR I SAW HIM!
ALEX... HURRY!!!

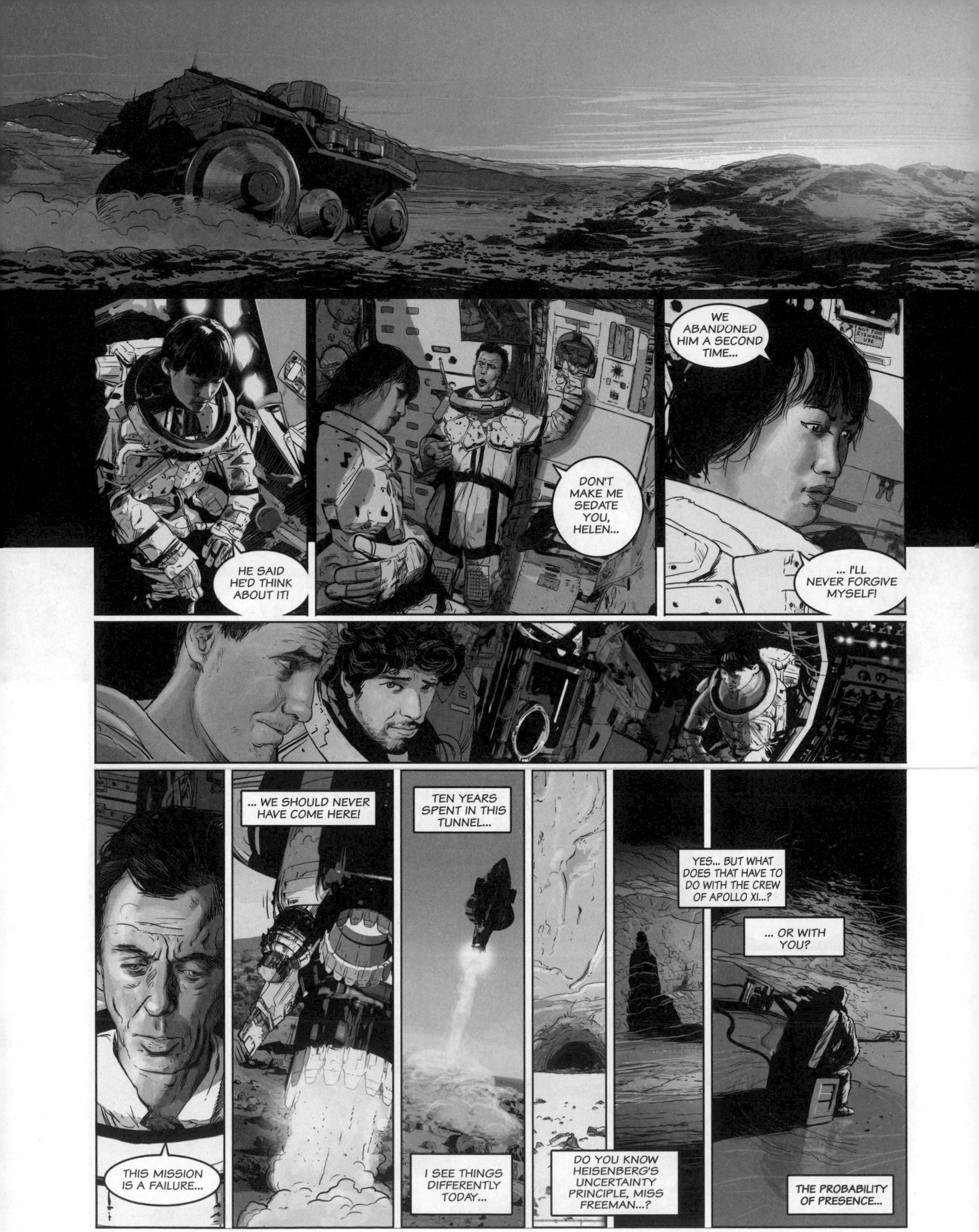
WE ABANDONED HIM A SECOND TIME...
DON'T MAKE ME SEDATE YOU, HELEN...
HE SAID HE'D THINK ABOUT IT!
... I'LL NEVER FORGIVE MYSELF!
THIS MISSION IS A FAILURE...
... WE SHOULD NEVER HAVE COME HERE!
TEN YEARS SPENT IN THIS TUNNEL...
I SEE THINGS DIFFERENTLY TODAY...
DO YOU KNOW HEISENBERG'S UNCERTAINTY PRINCIPLE, MISS FREEMAN...?
YES... BUT WHAT DOES THAT HAVE TO DO WITH THE CREW OF APOLLO XI...?
... OR WITH YOU?
THE PROBABILITY OF PRESENCE...

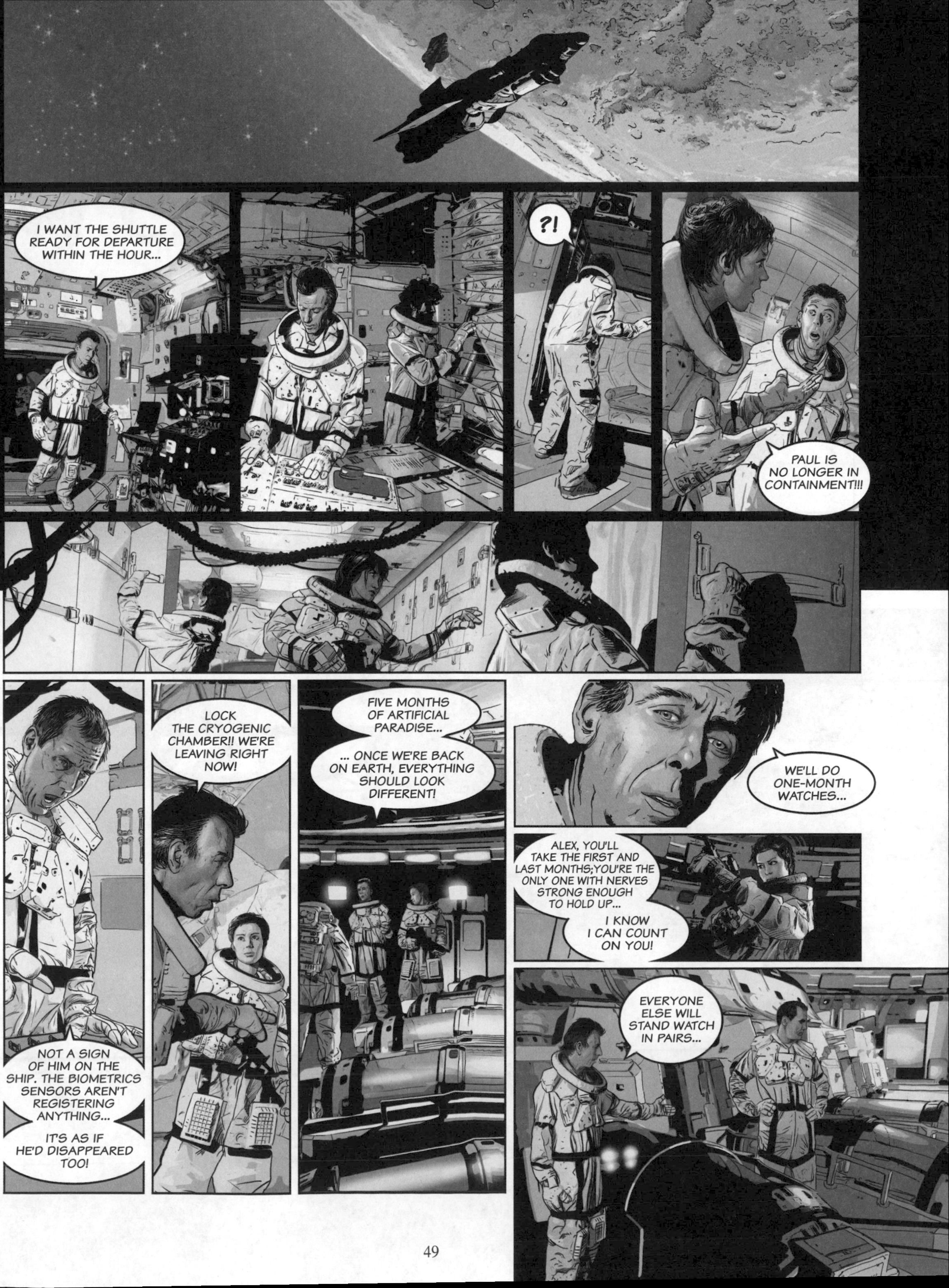
I WANT THE SHUTTLE READY FOR DEPARTURE WITHIN THE HOUR...
?!
PAUL IS NO LONGER IN CONTAINMENT!!!
NOT A SIGN OF HIM ON THE SHIP. THE BIOMETRICS SENSORS AREN'T REGISTERING ANYTHING...
IT'S AS IF HE'D DISAPPEARED TOO!
LOCK THE CRYOGENIC CHAMBER!! WE'RE LEAVING RIGHT NOW!
FIVE MONTHS OF ARTIFICIAL PARADISE...
... ONCE WE'RE BACK ON EARTH, EVERYTHING SHOULD LOOK DIFFERENT!
WE'LL DO ONE-MONTH WATCHES...
ALEX, YOU'LL TAKE THE FIRST AND LAST MONTHS;YOU'RE THE ONLY ONE WITH NERVES STRONG ENOUGH TO HOLD UP...
I KNOW I CAN COUNT ON YOU!
EVERYONE ELSE WILL STAND WATCH IN PAIRS...

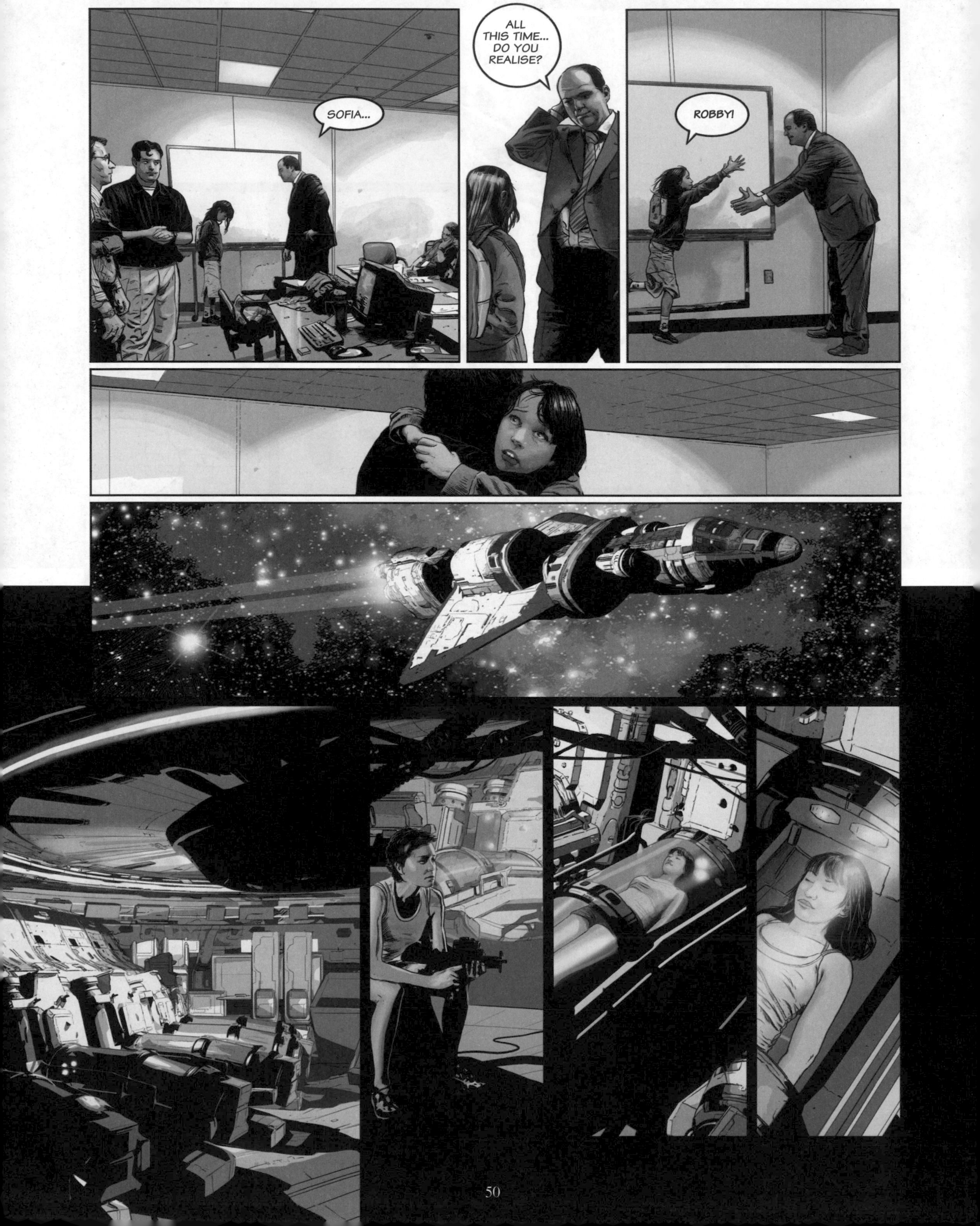
SOFIA...
ALL THIS TIME... DO YOU REALISE?
ROBBY!

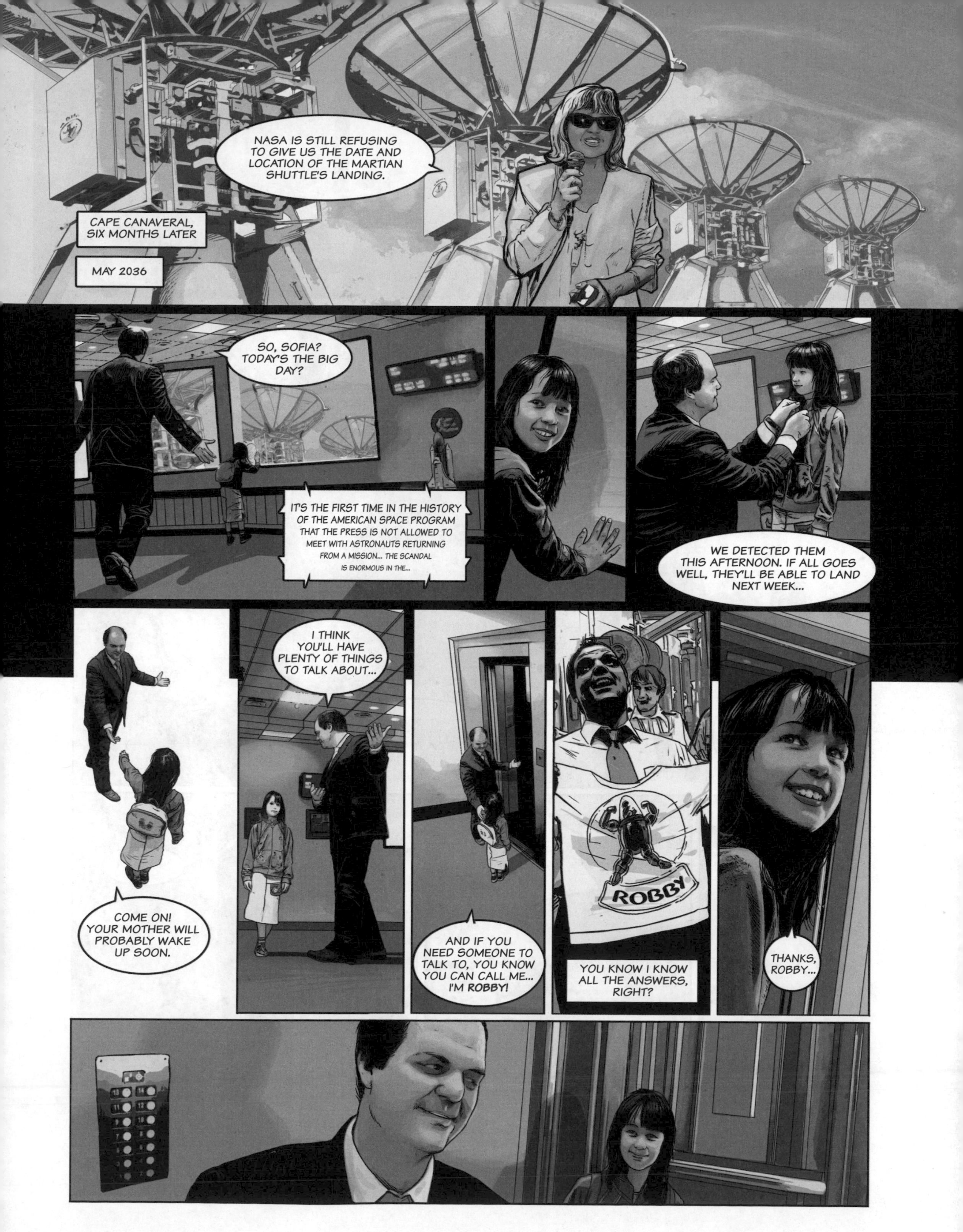

NASA IS STILL REFUSING TO GIVE US THE DATE AND LOCATION OF THE MARTIAN SHUTTLE'S LANDING.
CAPE CANAVERAL, SIX MONTHS LATER
MAY 2036
SO, SOFIA? TODAY'S THE BIG DAY?
IT'S THE FIRST TIME IN THE HISTORY OF THE AMERICAN SPACE PROGRAM THAT THE PRESS IS NOT ALLOWED TO MEET WITH ASTRONAUTS RETURNING FROM A MISSION... THE SCANDAL IS ENORMOUS IN THE...
WE DETECTED THEM THIS AFTERNOON. IF ALL GOES WELL, THEY'LL BE ABLE TO LAND NEXT WEEK...
COME ON! YOUR MOTHER WILL PROBABLY WAKE UP SOON.
I THINK YOU'LL HAVE PLENTY OF THINGS TO TALK ABOUT...
AND IF YOU NEED SOMEONE TO TALK TO, YOU KNOW YOU CAN CALL ME... I'M ROBBY!
ROBBY
YOU KNOW I KNOW ALL THE ANSWERS, RIGHT?
THANKS, ROBBY...

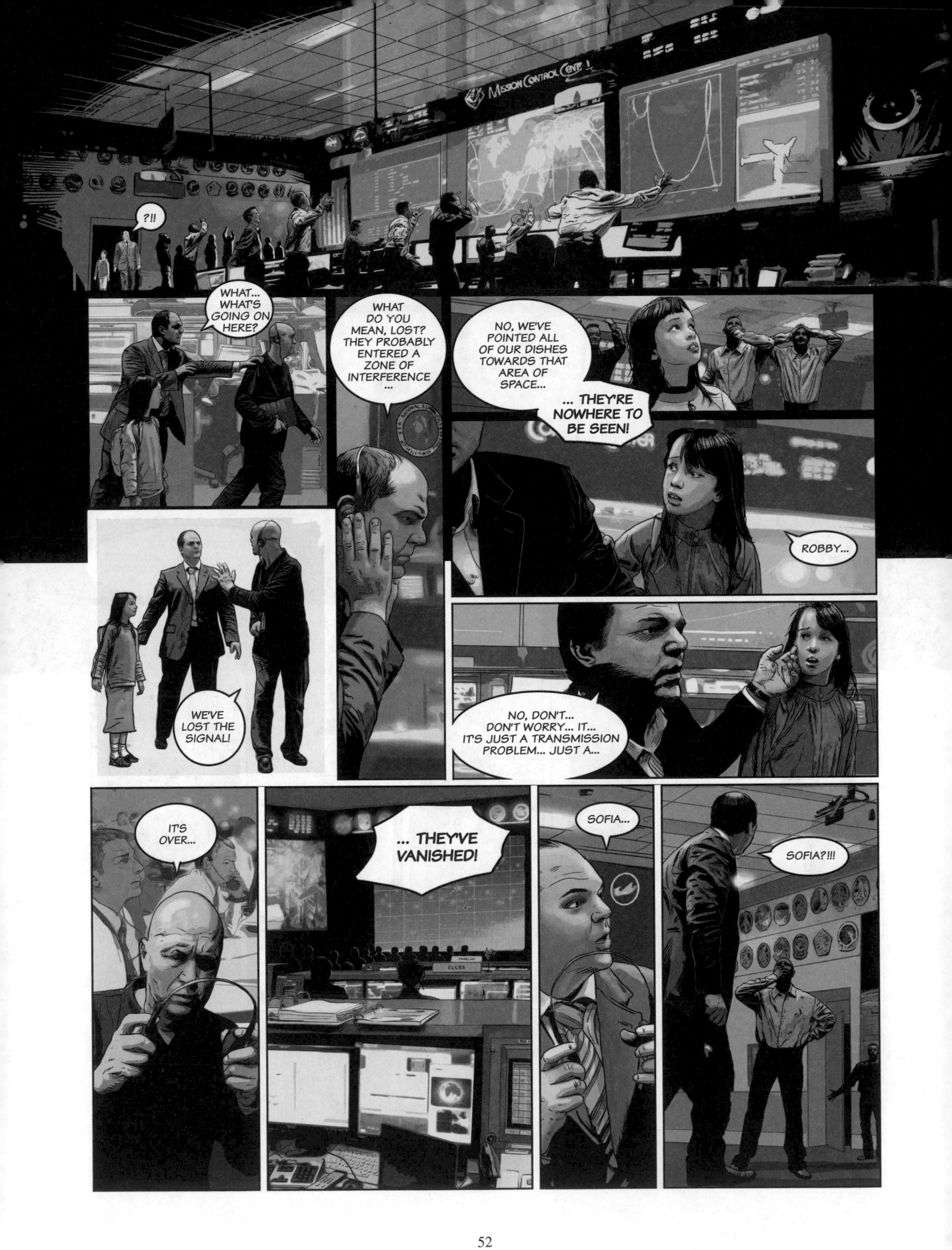
MISSION CONTROL CENTER
?!!
WHAT... WHAT'S GOING ON HERE?
WE'VE LOST THE SIGNAL!
WHAT DO YOU MEAN, LOST? THEY PROBABLY ENTERED A ZONE OF INTERFERENCE ...
NO, WE'VE POINTED ALL OF OUR DISHES TOWARDS THAT AREA OF SPACE...
... THEY'RE NOWHERE TO BE SEEN!
ROBBY...
NO, DON'T... DON'T WORRY... IT... IT'S JUST A TRANSMISSION PROBLEM... JUST A...
IT'S OVER...
... THEY'VE VANISHED!
SOFIA...
SOFIA?!!!

HELEN...

WAKE UP... IT... IT'S UNBELIEVABLE!

ALEKS... ALEKSA? IS... IS THAT YOU? WHAT'S...

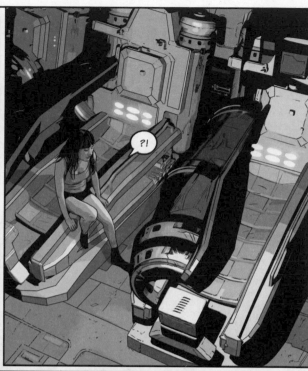

?!

DAMMIT! BUT THAT'S IMPOSSIBLE!

WE'RE SCREWED! WE'RE ALL SCREWED!!!

WHAT'S GOING ON?

THERE'S NO... DOUBT ANY-MORE, KURT?

I CHECKED SEVERAL TIMES IN MANUAL MODE. IT'S NOT A CALCULATION ERROR.

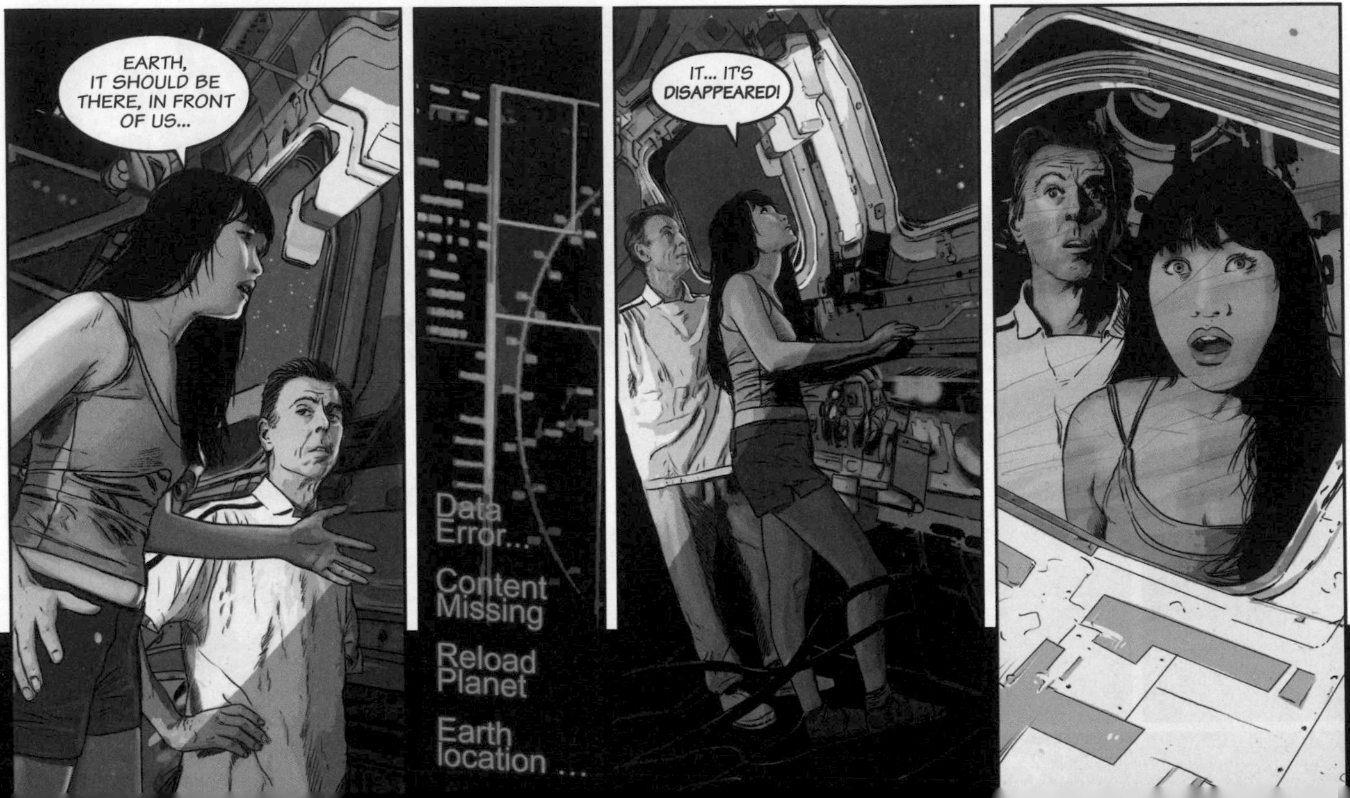
EARTH, IT SHOULD BE THERE, IN FRONT OF US...
Data Error...
Content Missing
Reload Planet
Earth location ...
IT... IT'S DISAPPEARED!

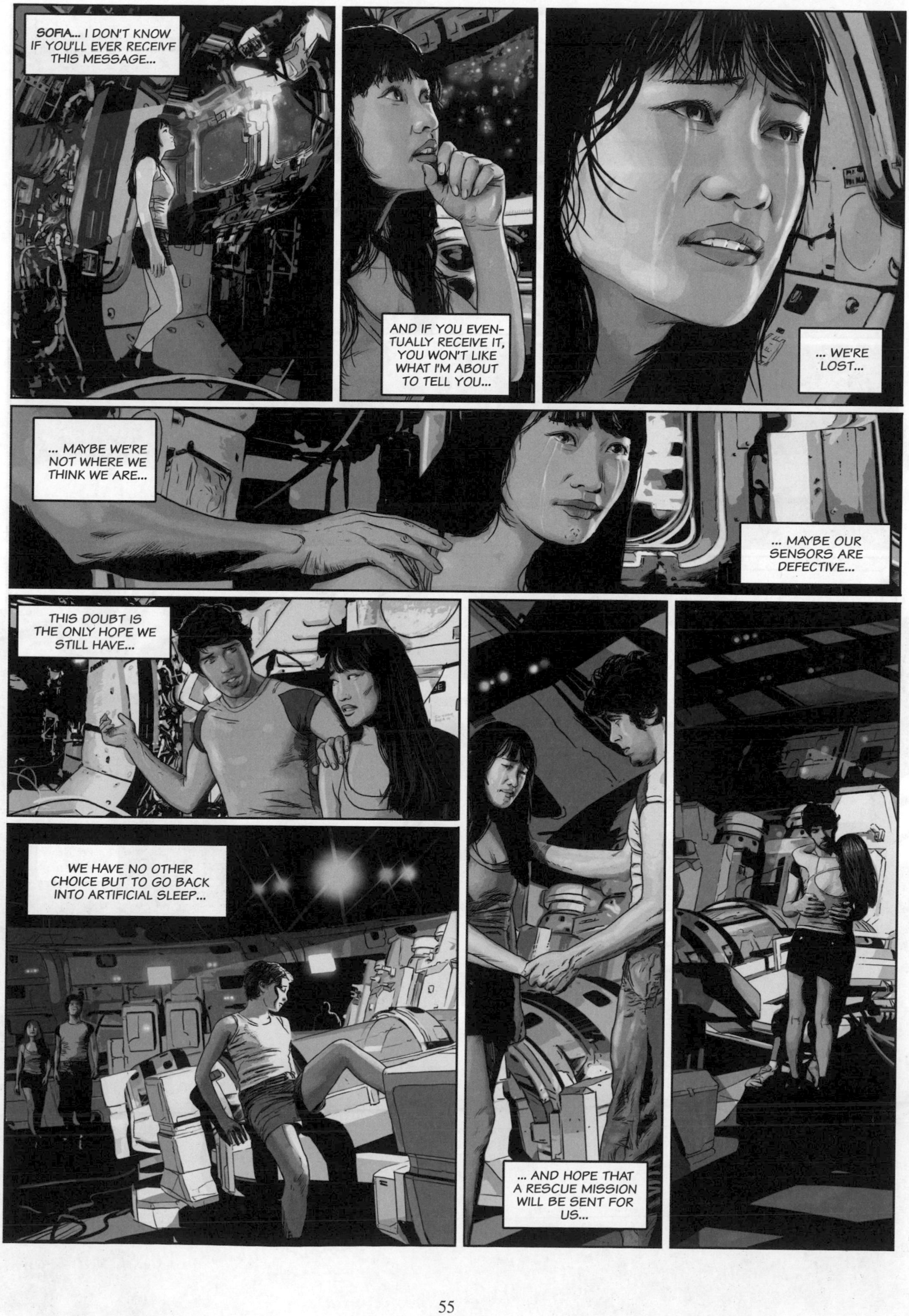
SOFIA... I DON'T KNOW IF YOU'LL EVER RECEIVF THIS MESSAGE...
AND IF YOU EVEN-TUALLY RECEIVE IT, YOU WON'T LIKE WHAT I'M ABOUT TO TELL YOU...
... WE'RE LOST...
... MAYBE WE'RE NOT WHERE WE THINK WE ARE...
... MAYBE OUR SENSORS ARE DEFECTIVE...
THIS DOUBT IS THE ONLY HOPE WE STILL HAVE...
WE HAVE NO OTHER CHOICE BUT TO GO BACK INTO ARTIFICIAL SLEEP...
... AND HOPE THAT A RESCUE MISSION WILL BE SENT FOR US...

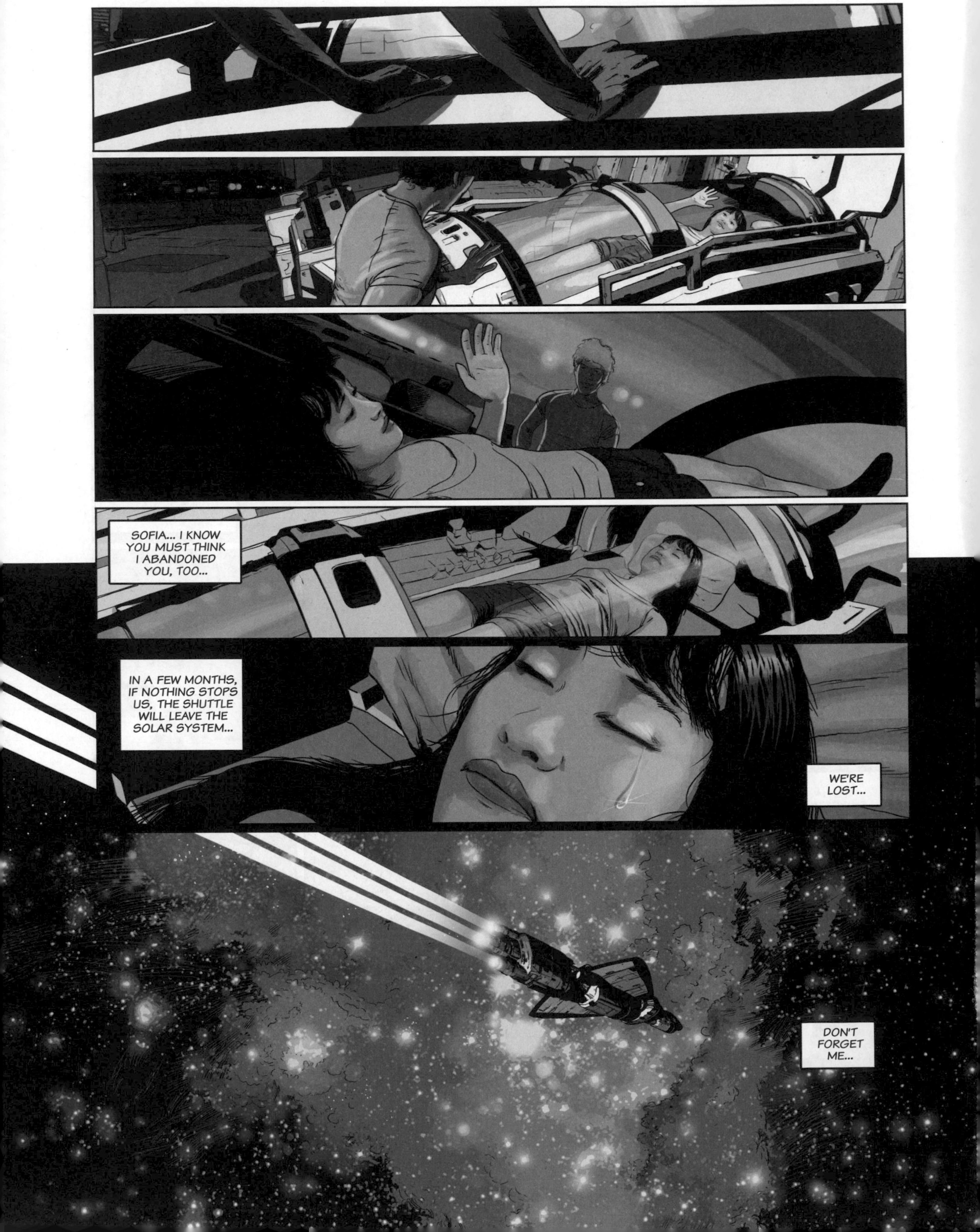
SOFIA... I KNOW YOU MUST THINK I ABANDONED YOU, TOO...
IN A FEW MONTHS, IF NOTHING STOPS US, THE SHUTTLE WILL LEAVE THE SOLAR SYSTEM...
WE'RE LOST...
DON'T FORGET ME...